"Combining interviews with both the late comedian and several key associates from his early life,
McCabe paints an even clearer picture of Stan's
formative years as an entertainer and screen comic
than emerged in *Mr. Laurel and Mr. Hardy*..."
— Leonard Maltin, film historian

THE
COMEDY
WORLD
OF
STAN
LAUREL

"Drawing on his own intimate friendship with
Laurel and that of his co-workers and relatives,
McCabe has crafted a loosely-knit documentary of
the personal life of the man he calls the 'most
creative member of the greatest comedy partnership in history.'"
— James Martin, *Chicago Sun-Times*

D1044571

THE COMEDY WORLD OF STAN LAUREL

JOHN McCABE

MOONSTONE PRESS

For IDA
and
all Sons of the Desert
everywhere

THE COMEDY WORLD OF STAN LAUREL
CENTENNIAL EDITION
Published by Moonstone Press,
P.O. Box 142, Beverly Hills CA 90213

Cover design by Jordan R. Young
Centenary logo by Barrie Finney
Frontispiece photo by Brown Meggs

Manufactured in the United States of America

Library of Congress Cataloging in Publication Data
McCabe, John, 1920-
    The comedy world of Stan Laurel / by John McCabe. — Rev. ed.
        p. cm.
    ISBN 0-940410-23-0 (alk. paper)
    ISBN 0-940410-22-2 (pbk.: alk. paper)
    1. Laurel, Stan.   2. Comedians—United States—Biography.
3. Motion picture actors and actresses—United States—Biography.
I. Title.
PN2287.L285M28   1990
791.43'028'092—dc820   90-34889
[B]   CIP

The paper used in this publication meets the minimum requirements of American National Standards for Information Sciences, Permanance of Paper for Printed Library Materials ANSI Z39.48-1984

10 9 8 7 6 5 4 3 2 1

Acknowledgments

My prime obligation for source material is to Ida Kitaeva Laurel, whose idea this book was, a lady who was born indelibly a giver as many are born to the other persuasion. I am also deeply grateful to G.M. "Broncho Billy" Anderson; Peter Bogdanovich; R.E. Braff; Frank Butler; George Burns; Larry Byrd; John "Pour" Carroll; Booth Colman; Alice Cooke; Joyce Dexter; Kent Eastin; Dolores Esposito, R.N., of the Sayville Nursing Home, Sayville, N.Y.; Bob Elliott; Joe Finck; Robert Fusillo; Billy and Ella Gilbert; Clarence "Stax" Graves of the Hal Roach Studios; Sir Alec Guinness; Tony and Lois Laurel Hawes; Jim Kerkoff; Bill Kennedy; Al Kilgore; David Larson; Glenn Laxton; Laine Liska; Mae Laurel; Jean "Babe" London; Mackinac College Library; George Marshall; Brown Meggs; Vija, Linny, Sean and Deirdre McCabe; Chuck McCann; Leo McCarey; Milo V. Olson; Mike Polacek; James Powers of the American Film Institute Center for Advanced Film Studies; Lucille Hardy Price; W.T. Rabe; Joe Rock; Tom Sefton; Ben and Ione Shipman; Randy Skretvedt; Alex Soma; Paul Toepp; Dick Van Dyke; Sam Vaughan, my former editor at Doubleday; Dan Waldron; Marc Wanamaker; and Jordan R. Young, who edited the centennial edition. Last, particular thanks to Dick Bann, who read my manuscript with the assiduity so deeply characteristic of all his researches into Laurel and Hardy fact and fancy.

Stan and Jack, Malibu, Calif. 1957. *Photo by Brown Meggs.*

About the Author

John McCabe enjoyed a close friendship with Stan Laurel, which inspired him to write *Mr. Laurel and Mr. Hardy*, the authorized biography of the beloved team, and three additional books: *Laurel & Hardy* (with Al Kilgore and Richard W. Bann); *The Comedy World of Stan Laurel*; and *Babe: The Life of Oliver Hardy*. In addition to ghost-writing James Cagney's autobiography, he is the author of *Charlie Chaplin*; *George M. Cohan: The Man Who Owned Broadway*; *The Grand Hotel*; and *Proclaiming the Word* (with G. B. Harrison). McCabe is the founding father of The Sons of the Desert, the international Laurel and Hardy appreciation society. He divides his time between homes in Brooklyn, New York, and Mackinac Island, Michigan, where he lives with his wife, former actress and one-time Laurel and Hardy co-star Rosina Lawrence.

Preface to 1990 Edition

Please indulge some personal history. As a child actor, I grew up revering John Barrymore instead of my contemporaries' idol, Babe Ruth. When I was 20, I met Barrymore and in a long chat we spoke of *our* mutual idol, Shakespeare. Barrymore, the greatest Hamlet of his day, in answer to my anxiously naive question on how best to act Shakespeare, gently questioned me about him. It became embarrassingly apparent that my knowledge of Shakespeare was sadly insubstantial.

That conversation of 1940 eventually led me to a Ph. D. at the Shakespeare Institute in Stratford-upon-Avon, England, and while there, to a fortuitous meeting with Laurel and Hardy in person at nearby Birmingham. Since then the teaching, directing and even acting of Shakespeare has been my blessedly happy lot. Also, in time's fullness I became the authorized biographer of Laurel and Hardy, and wrote four books about them.

All this came to mind recently when an old friend asked why I had divided my life into such widely divergent enthusiasms. "Simple," I said. "Because they aren't widely divergent at all. Shakespeare and Laurel and Hardy are cut from the same bolt of cloth. The three show us life's follies, and in seeing them we find our own, and so laugh warmly at ourselves."

I went on to explain to my friend that Shakespeare even created a number of comedy characters just like Laurel and Hardy — Sir Andrew Aguecheek and Dogberry come first to mind — men just as comically dense as Stan and Ollie, replete with malapropisms and silly ponderings. Years before, I told this to Stan, who was delighted. "Blimey!" he said with mock hauteur in affected upper class accent. "Our old pal, Shakespeare. Three of a kind!"

In *Much Ado About Nothing*, Shakespeare has the vacant-minded constable, Dogberry, arraign a pair of criminals before a town clerk. "Is our whole dissembly appeared?" asks the constable, and since they seem to be, he first asks the pair, in custom of the time, if they serve God. They reply they hope they do. Dogberry then fussily instructs the clerk (who is writing out the charge): "Write down that they hope they serve God; and write God *first*, for God defend but God should go before such villains!" This, surely, is seventeenth century Laurel and Hardy, both of whom by the way would have been superb as Dogberry. Instances of this kind abound in Shakespeare, and I would periodically type out such scenes and send them to Stan. In our next phone conversation he would read me a climactic line or two in his screen character's voice, and we would both laugh uproariously. There was never any false modesty about Stan. A genius knows his own worth. That's why he's a genius.

Rereading *The Comedy World of Stan Laurel* after all these years in this fine new edition has put me again in touch with that genius. I am indebted to Jordan Young and Moonstone Press for the chance, and to Tony and Lois Laurel Hawes for the use of much precious memorabilia, which appears in print for the first time.

So — now that I enter the cloistered shade of old age, those three great artists, Shakespeare, Stan Laurel and Oliver Hardy remain my constant and greatest joy. And so it shall be to the end.

John McCabe
Mackinac Island, Michigan
1990

Introduction

This is a documentary. It is both the memory of a man by a few of his friends and an informal look at his prime function in life. These pages partake of biography only in that those events in Stan Laurel's life which have not been previously recorded in the authorized biography, my *Mr. Laurel and Mr. Hardy,** are set down and more deeply assessed in terms of his unique personality than the first book's format allowed. Those readers unfamiliar with the earlier book will not be disadvantaged; they will find here a basic history of Laurel and Hardy's partnership and its genesis.

The personal memories of Stan Laurel I offer are those which illuminate to the degree I can his fascinating self and his justifiable obsession with laughter. Of his personality— his warm, rollicking spirit—I cannot hope to speak with full objectivity at all times, and if I do not, let this be apologetic forewarning. The fact is I loved the man this side idolatry and not, I think, without reason. In the twelve years of our friendship, there was not an occasion—either when we met or talked by telephone or corresponded—when I did not come away from the encounter infinitely the better for it.

*First published by Doubleday in 1961; reissued by Plume (New American Library) in 1985.

Introduction

Somewhat like Browning's duchess, Stan had a heart soon made glad, and that is how he affected those who knew him well—and those who didn't know him well. As to who he was, he was a man who existed almost solely for laughter. This, if anything, was the real Stan Laurel, and in probing talks with his widow, Ida, the person who knew him better than anyone in the world, that description has been amply confirmed.

This book is inevitably a miscellany. Fittingly, because that was Stan's approach to comedy. His comedic concepts were never tidily arranged in his own mind, as he was often to remark. He disliked generalizations on comedy in the main, and one looks with difficulty for prime themes or essential strands of idea in his notes, scripts, or story discussions with the gag men and directors he worked with through the years.

To illustrate. One afternoon I was reading to him a particularly arcane bit of analysis of the comedy of his old friend, Charlie Chaplin. It was written by a much-respected film scholar. After a few paragraphs of this recondite palaver, Stan interrupted me with impatience. "That kind of junk annoys the hell out of me," he said. "What people like that don't understand and never will understand is that what we were trying to do was to make people laugh in as many ways as we could, without trying to prove a point or show the world its troubles or get into some deep meaning. Why the hell do you have to explain why a thing is funny? We were trying to do a very simple thing, give people some laughs, and that's *all* we were trying to do."

Although I agreed with every word he said, I attempted to

present to him objectively what I thought might be the rationale for those film critics who find in great film comedy the troubles of the world turned arsy-varsy. "These people," I said, "see Chaplin, Keaton, Langdon, Fields, Laurel and Hardy and the Marx Brothers as telling basic truths about mankind. They consider great comedy films as a kind of happy onslaught on the things that are wrong in our society. For this reason the critics think it important to assess that comedy in terms of society. Don't you think comedy *can* help us find what's wrong with the world?"

"Certainly," Stan said, "if we were George Bernard Shaw or Shakespeare. If you think for one minute that Charlie ever sat down and thought to himself 'Ah, ha! This is going to tell what's wrong with society!' you're wrong. He sat down to make people laugh and that's *all* he did. Just like me, Charlie's no intellectual, you know, no matter how brilliant he is—and in my opinion *no* one is more brilliant than Charlie—at making people *laugh*. That was his job; that was my job, and that's all we were good for. Charlie and Buster and Harry Langdon, Fields, and us—we were just doing as many good gags as we could. We weren't trying to change the world, or what the hell have you.

"Anyone who thinks *Modern Times* has got a big message is just putting it there himself. Charlie knew that the pressures of modern life and factory life would be good for a lot of *laughs*, and that's why he did the film—not because he wanted to diagnose the industrial revolution or some goddamned thing." (*Laughter.*) "I never saw *Monsieur Verdoux* or *The King in New York*. But as I understand it, they were serious films to begin with, not pure comedies, and *The Great Dictator* was lousy in the serious parts. I don't think Charlie would try to put a message in a pure comedy. At the risk of repeating myself, we were just trying to make people laugh. Some people just don't believe that. They think deep down we all put some kind of bloody message in our films. Well, they're wrong. We were having fun and trying to *give* a little fun."

Assessing that fun is part of this book but it will not be an extensive evaluation because I believe, as Stan did, that pulling comedy apart not only diminishes it in vital respects but is pretty boring into the bargain.

Those readers wishing detailed accounts of how Laurel and Hardy met, were joined together, formulated their comedic style and experienced thirty lively years together are referred to my *Mr. Laurel and Mr. Hardy*. The present book is devoted principally to the more fully creative member of that partnership. As the principal idea man for the team, as the chief programmer of their gags and stories, Stan deserves (I believe) this special tribute to his high professionalism, a tribute which will let him speak as much as possible for himself. He certainly shall speak in his own tongue with the printing in these pages of the scripts which he wrote for Laurel and Hardy stage tours both in the United States and the British Isles. Moreover, it gives me deep pleasure to be able to publish an outline, together with a few of the gags he had crafted, for one of the Laurel and Hardy television films which were to begin shooting a few days before Oliver Hardy was felled by the stroke which ended his working days forever.

From these variegated materials will come into general focus, I think, the comedy world of Stan Laurel as adequately as the printed word can represent it. But that is inadequate, of course. Ultimately, his world can only be found in the living laughter of those who see his films. That is the true testament of his genius, which is just how he wanted it. I have often thought what a deep joy it is that Laurel and Hardy did their work in films instead of in the theatre as, at times, they were tempted to do. It means, blessedly, that we have them forever.

Arthur Stanley Jefferson and his actress-mother, Madge Metcalfe, circa 1897.

One

Among Stan's papers after his death, I found an engaging
document written by his father, Arthur J. Jefferson, known
to his contemporaries as "A.J." This splendidly overwritten
memoir of his son was A.J.'s attempt to get back in what he
called "the writing game"—a game he had engaged in during
his years in Northern England and Scotland as theatre lessee,
manager, comedian, and playwright. Stan's mother was Madge
Metcalfe, A.J.'s helpmeet in many ways, who was the leading
actress in the Jefferson companies which toured the English
provinces during the turn of this century.

A.J.'s biography of Stan was written in 1939 at the height
of Stan's fame, and the old gentleman was determined that
it see print. Stan gently discouraged the project because the
document was written in florid Victorian style covering rather
less than a third of Stan's life, and was interspersed with
windy disquisitions on irrelevant matters like A.J.'s trip to
Canada following a visit with Stan in 1936. What this mini-
biography (titled *Turning the Pages*) holds of value is the
telling of a few engrossing stories of Stan's childhood. A few
excerpts from *Turning the Pages* give some pleasant insights
into Stan's earliest years.

A.J.:

"Stan was born in Ulverston, Lancashire, June 16, 1890, at the home of his grandmother—a dear 'little old lady' of fragrant memory—who, due to his mother's protracted illness following his birth, 'mothered' him until he was about five or six, when she brought him to our home in North Shields —where, incidentally, I was controlling the local Theatre Royal and various other theatres in nearby districts, and touring various plays (dramas) written by myself. I mention these facts merely because they, fairly obviously, have a bearing on Stan's ultimate choice of a career.

"As Stan grew older, it became increasingly apparent that his young mind was obsessed with the idea of one day 'following in father's footsteps'; spending all his pocket money on toy theatres, Punch and Judy shows, marionettes, shadowgraphs [actors posing behind illuminated screens], magic lanterns, etc.—*anything* providing scope for entertainment."

A.J. then writes at tedious length of Stan's brother, Gordon, and his sister, Olga, and their "enamorment of the stage," together with Gordon's ultimate success as a theatre manager and Olga's retirement, despite her skill in playing "Delilah-type" roles, into marriage.* He goes on:

"But to resume my narrative: when about nine years of age, Stan begged me to convert the attic of our home in North Shields—exceptionally large and suited for the pur-

---

* Stan had another brother, Teddy, not at all interested in show business, who revered automobiles. He worked contentedly as Stan's chauffeur for years. Teddy died, incredibly, in a dental chair—the victim, Stan told me, of a mis-diagnosis.

pose—into a miniature theatre, to which I agreed, calling upon my local theatre staff to carry out the work (in which they evinced great interest)—producing very creditable results: stage, proscenium, wings, etc. and footlights (the latter being oil lamps with reflectors—safer than gas, we thought). With seating for about 20 to 30 people: in brief, a perfect replica of the average small theatre at that period. Stan, assisted by several 'dying to act' boys and girls, was hard at work inaugurating the 'Stanley Jefferson Amateur Dramatic Society'—featuring said S.J. as Director, Manager, Stage Manager, Author, Producer, and Leading Man."

Stan wrote a series of roles for himself, A.J. said, which combined both heroism and comedy. As to admission fee:

". . . when cash was not available, subscriptions were payable in kind: any articles useful in the general staging effects—carpets, rugs, curtains, crockery and domestic articles in general suitable as stage props. Concerning these non-cash contributions, it happened that the boy selected to enact the villain parts—by name, Harold, son of a local butcher—had nothing to offer except two white mice which Stan accepted mainly due to the fact that Harold's features (of the bulldog type) insured not only giving due effect to the many 'curse yer's' lavishly interposed in villain's parts but also guaranteed acceleration of sympathy for the heroics of the leading man—which Stan had piled up for his own declamation. Promotion details being completed, and the cast selected, rehearsals commenced in real earnest of a play (written of course by Stan) with a plot which was a flagrant copy of various plays, including some of my own, which he

3

had witnessed at various of the theatres I had managed through the years.

"I forget the play's title but it was abnormally bloodthirsty, introducing as its program stated, 'Excitement! Struggles! And *murders!*' Stan, of course, being the one who tracked down the assassin and brought him to justice. At length after very full rehearsals, and the Hon. Sec'y of the Society having duly extended written notices of the opening night date, price of tickets, etc., to all in the neighborhood likely to be interested, the eventful night arrived. There was a very satisfactory response from the neighborhood. Every seat (any shortage in that direction resulted in a remorseless foray by Stan and his assistants on every room in the house) was occupied—by an expectant and acutely interested audience. That audience saw many of their own familiar household articles on stage, of course. Old home week as it were!

"Following a brilliant selection by the orchestra (a musical box emitting what was evidently intended to be the tune 'Blue Bells of Scotland,' unfortunately not heard beyond the first row of seats), the curtain rose, and the play commenced—each performer receiving rapturous applause as he or she made his or her entrance, the density of the ovation depending largely upon the numerical strength of the parental cliques involved—Stan being especially honored—probably due to the fact of its being an open secret that he occasionally distributed free passes to my theatre, the Theatre Royal, to his favored friends.

"The first act, ending with Stan's oath to 'track the monster to his lair' evoked tumultuous applause and quivering excitement. The second act during which Stan true to his oath 'cornered his prey' called upon that monster to surrender, which the said villain denounced by Stan as the 'epitome of all the vices' laughed to scorn. The second act ended in a life or death struggle, rousing the audience to a high pitch of excitement, the parents taking sides with their respective offspring, and the juvenile females with the boy they favored most. The audience egged the actors on with cries of 'Stick it, Stan!' or 'Good lad, Harold!' (Stan had lifted this fight bodily from the famous fight in the late John Lawson's—of beloved memory—play, *Only a Jew,* the great fight between the Jew and the Gentile.) Stan and Harold threw missiles, anything handy and some of them quite foreign to the environment at each other; then they cast off their outer garments in the struggle; clinched several times followed by a joint fall, and then came the stereotyped rolling and rolling over the stage, backwards, then forwards! (Note: In the 'good old days of the drama,' no struggle was acclaimed by the gallery unless accompanied by the contestants adopting these tactics, the number of rolls depending on the prolongation of applause.)

"But there was an unexpected climax to this fight. Stan and Harold threshed and kicked about so strongly that they knocked over one of the paraffin oil lamp footlights and within seconds the side curtains which were of very flimsy fabric were blazing furiously! This caused a state of panic among the audience, some of whom made valiant efforts to tear the curtains down. Now, it so happened that an urgent business appointment in Newcastle in connection with my theatres had prevented my being present to compère the opening proceedings. (I heard about all this later on.) I arrived just at this exciting moment. On opening the door to the room I heard shrieks and the cries of 'Fire!' and I was almost knocked over by the excited throng as they trooped down the staircase. Picking up one of the chemical fire extinguishers which I had about the house, I dashed up and succeeded in quenching the flames, which by this time had got hold of the wooden framework of the stage. Calm being restored, a roll call confirmed that only Stan and Harold had suffered any burns. Genuine troupers both, the boys had continued their mighty struggle all the way through the fire, and were totally oblivious to the flames which were surrounding them! They persevered in their fight until pulled apart by their respective mothers. Soon afterwards, amidst regrets, expressions of sympathy and handshakes, our audience dispersed. My doctor was called and outside of singed eyebrows, Harold was fine, and was forthwith despatched by cab to his home.

"But poor old Stan! He had suffered more than a few burns. His grief at the play's ending was truly tragic but a good night's rest seemed to restore him to normal, and indeed his superficial burns were quite soon healed. However, there was still trouble a-brewing. A few days later, Stan received a severe letter from Harold blaming Stan for the loss of his eyebrows and also demanding the return of his subscription —the aforesaid two white mice. Stan naturally held entirely opposite views and he consulted me about how he should deal with the matter. I reminded him that a soft answer, as the old saying goes, turneth away wrath, and I advised a diplomatic letter to Harold, suggesting that Stan let me see the letter before posting. This was the result:

Ayton House
North Shields

Dear Harold:

I think it is very unkind of you to write me like this. The fire was all your fault; if you had let go of my throat when you saw my face going all red, we shouldn't have rolled over as far as the lamps. You have lost nothing over the accident. *I* have lost my *theatre*. Dad is having it all done away with for good and all—and all my pocket money since it started. I am sorry about your eyebrows being burned off, of course, but they will grow again. And don't forget that *I* got some nasty burns too—as well as being nearly strangled to death by you.

You once told me that the men in your father's slaughterhouse had once let you help them to kill a pig. I didn't believe you then but I do now. In fact, after the way you tried to kill me, I should believe you now if you told me that you had killed a cow all by yourself.

Stanley

"Disapproving of that final sentence in the letter, I insisted upon its cancellation, insisting that he should hold out the olive branch. Consequently, in place of the offending sentence, Stan wrote: 'I cannot agree to returning your two white mice but I'll tell you what I will do. If they get married and have babies, I will divide them with you. If you want to be friends I do, if you don't, I don't. Stanley.'"

A.J. was unable to remember if the white mice ever

cohabited profitably but he was certain that the Stanley Jefferson Amateur Dramatic Society was no more. It was, said the old man, "consigned to the limbo of defeated aspirations." Once in response to a question of mine, "Were you always interested in comedy?" Stan gave an interesting reply.

Stan:

"Always. Even as a little kid. I can remember just as clearly as yesterday when I was at school in Bishop Auckland a certain teacher named Bates. It was a boarding school, and after the kids had gone to bed, Bates would come and take me into his private study where he and a couple of other masters were relaxing—with a bottle. Bates would then have me entertain them with jokes, imitations, what the hell have you—anything for a laugh. I must have been awful but they seemed to get a big kick out of it, and I played many return engagements there.

"I can't remember now mostly what I did but I certainly had this talent for clowning right from the beginning, more or less. I don't think playing to Bates and the other masters helped my education any as I was given a lot of privileges—and a lot of my backwardness in class was overlooked which many times since I've regretted. As it happened, my career turned out well but once in a while I wonder what would have happened if I had been a good student. Perhaps I might have been a better comedian if I had been better in the book-learning department.

"Anyway, those were happy days at Bishop Auckland.

I remember one of those teachers—a German, and naturally he was the German master—who didn't seem to like me at all. He had the habit of carrying a pencil crosswise in his mouth, and when I couldn't answer his questions in class, he used to go into a frenzy. He'd chew that pencil up into pieces and spit them out of his mouth in disgust. One night in Bates's study I was stuck for something to do, so unfortunately I gave an imitation of the German master and his pencil-chewing business. This killed Bates who demanded I do it over and over again. Well, the German master was present, and it sure didn't kill him! Naturally I hadn't meant to antagonize him, but he really became my enemy after that. What I did I did trying to make the masters enjoy themselves. Anything for a laugh!"

Stan's appearance before the Bates coterie whetted his appearance for larger audiences. His dad's manuscript continues the story.

A.J.:

"During August 1901, I took over a long lease of the Metropole Theatre, Glasgow. This was formerly the old Scotia Music Hall famed now as the starting point in the career of Sir Harry Lauder, but which was in 1901 newly rebuilt on modern lines. This new lease demanded my full personal attention so I moved my family from North Shields to Glasgow, and it henceforth became my headquarters for the next twenty-three years. Meanwhile Stan had grown apace and upon the completion of his schooling, it was arranged that he should take up duties at the 'Met,' as my theatre was popularly known locally. I wanted Stan to qualify first as the Met's assistant manager, and ultimately its manager.

"But it was soon apparent that the seeds of Stan's ambition which had been sown in North Shields and Bishop Auckland to become an actor were still actively germinating. He performed his business duties at the Met satisfactorily but he had no real heart interest in the business side of the curtain. In his spare time and without my knowledge he had written himself a comedy music hall monologue, and, again without my knowledge, had prevailed upon a friend of mine, proprietor of a music hall in the city, to give him an opening date for a trial show.

"Before I left home that eventful night, Stan asked me to release him from duty, having been invited to a party, to which I naturally assented. As the show at the Met began that night, it was a very fine evening I remember, and for some incredible reason I decided to take a stroll. What moved me to do so I cannot imagine, for from my earliest days in management, I had and have always adopted the policy of always being on the spot in my theatres, ready for any emergency. It may have been telepathic contact with Stan; I cannot say—but whatever the explanation, I answered the call of my whim, and strange to relate, my footsteps led me in the direction of my friend's [Albert E. Pickard] music hall. We hadn't met for quite a long time, and on my arrival he was standing in front of the hall. After the usual greeting, he said, 'You're just in time. Stan is due on in about five minutes.'

"My amazement needs no stressing. However, I didn't give it away (my friend thought I knew all about Stan's appearance), and we went in and sat in the front stalls. Very soon Stan's number, billed as an 'extra turn,' went up. On he came wearing a pair of baggy patched trousers (new trousers of *mine,* cut down, patches added), and also my best frock coat and silk hat. (Known as a 'topper' in those days.) He did his act, the details of which I cannot now remember, and he got a very good reception and scored a genuine success, finishing up to loud laughter and applause and even shouts of 'Encore!' The shouts brought him back, and he beamed the now popular Laurel smile, but in bowing his acknowledgments, he spotted me!

"Giving a subdued yell of horrified astonishment, he dropped my topper which thereupon rolled toward the footlights. Stan pursued it, tried to grab it and in so doing kicked it accidentally into the orchestra where one of the musicians made a rush to retrieve it and stepped on it, squashing it thoroughly! Then Stan made a dash for the exit but his luck was out. As he ran off he came in contact with a steel hook fixed in the wings for a trapeze act and the hook ripped off half the skirt of my beautiful frock coat. Exit . . . loud applause! My music hall friend was greatly pleased with the act. He said that the 'business' of smashing the topper and the tearing of the coat was extremely funny! Groaning inwardly, I departed for the Met, feeling certain that Stan, who was always a very plucky kid, would return and face the music. He did—*very* forlorn, very apprehensive of the reception that he would get from me. Imagine, therefore, his astonishment and joy when I received him with open arms and congratulations and promises to help him achieve his ambition."

It was, in truth, one of the greatest moments in Stan's life and he was not ashamed to weep in gratitude and relief. A.J. began to cast about for means to help Stan become a performer. There was little for Stan in A.J.'s own company because the Jefferson theatrical companies specialized in melodramas not far removed in plot and tone from the play Stan had written for himself in North Shields. In any case, Stan had tasted the fullness of laughter and it became from that time the theme of his life.

In 1932, Stan was asked by the publicity department of Hal Roach Studios to write a biography for their use. This document which outlines his professional life he titled *Theatrical Career of Stan Laurel*. In it, he told of his experiences as a young comedian, beginning with the adventure in Pickard's Music Hall in Glasgow and his dad's pleasure with the act.

Stan:

"But Dad thought I wasn't experienced enough yet to branch out as a single, and suggested I'd be better off with some comedy company, playing strictly comedy parts. He then secured me an engagement with a very famous company, namely, Levy and Cardwell's Juvenile Pantomimes who produced shows similar to the satirical and clean burlesque shows in the U.S., only the actors were all youngsters, aged six to eighteen. This was burlesque in the old sense of the word—where you satirized a well-known story. I remained with the company for two seasons playing comedy parts and also became assistant stage manager. When the show closed after the second season, I rearranged a new single act and branched out in vaudeville, playing in small English variety houses. During this time my dad produced a successful vaudeville sketch, *Home from the Honeymoon,** which was played in the big time houses (Moss Empire's). After several weeks run he had trouble with one of the comedians in the sketch, so he replaced him with me for the balance of the season."

Stan played in his dad's sketch until a prominent musical comedy producer of the day, Edwin Marris, gave him a contract to appear in the vital role of the stable boy in a hit production, *Gentleman Jockey*. Following this and another engagement as the comedian in a melodrama entitled *Alone in the World,* Stan made another and very momentous change.

Stan:

"I returned to vaudeville again as a single act when I was scouted by a very famous comedy producer, Fred Karno. In his company was Charlie Chaplin who was their principal comedian. After I was with this company a couple of months Karno sent down a script for a new show he wanted to produce with the company the following Monday in London. We were all given our parts; Chaplin, of course, had the star part. We immediately went into rehearsal, and towards the end of the week Karno came personally to witness a re-

---

* Which Stan was later to transmute into the hilarious Laurel and Hardy three-reeler, *Another Fine Mess* (1930).

hearsal. This production was *Jimmy the Fearless*. At the last minute Chaplin told Karno he didn't like the show and refused to open in it. Karno then picked me out of the troupe and gave me the part, which I rehearsed Saturday and Monday, and opened in London on Monday night.

"The show was a terrific hit. Chaplin sat in front and watched my performance for one whole week, then decided he would play the part. I still continued with the troupe playing second comedian, also understudying Chaplin in a repertoire of about ten Karno shows. In 1910, the troupe was booked to play in America."

Billed as "Fred Karno's Comedians," the group opened in New York in an act called *The Wow-wows*, a burlesque on the initiation ceremonies of a typical fraternal order. *The Wow-wows* was not particularly successful, as Chaplin had warned Karno, but the tremendous pantomimic skills of the Englishmen more than offset the inadequacy of the material and the Karno group was engaged for a tour of the prestigious Sullivan and Considine vaudeville circuit across the United States. On this tour they played the actionful *A Night in an English Music Hall*, a broad satirization of English variety acts, which gave Chaplin the chance to show off his talents at their brightest. Stan at this time had asked Karno for a raise in salary, and upon refusal, left for home where he wrote a sketch, *The Rum 'Uns from Rome* which he played with various partners to indifferent success in England and on the Continent.

In 1912, the Karno troupe was re-engaged to tour the United States on the Sullivan-Considine circuit and Stan was hired again as Chaplin's understudy with the raise he

A young comic addicted to the roar of the greasepaint.

Boy comedian, Scotland, circa 1906.

Mr. and Mrs. H. B. LEVY'S COMPANIES.

Memorandum of Agreement made this *1st* day of

July. 190*7* between MR. AND MRS. HAROLD B. LEVY, Theatrical Managers of the one part, and *Mr Arthur Jefferson of Glasgow being guardian of Stanley Jefferson* of the other part.

WHEREAS the said MR. AND MRS. HAROLD B. LEVY agree to engage, and the said *Stanley Jefferson* agrees to accept an engagement at a salary of £ *Supplement from aug to Xmas and from Xmas to Easter* / : — weekly, to include all performances and matinees and to play the parts allotted them including specialities.

The said engagement to begin on or about *August 19th 1907*.

and to be for the Tour from *August 19th* to *Easter 1908 Inclusive*

Rehearsals to be given for two weeks commencing *August 12th* the said

Stanley Jefferson further agreeing to provide all dresses wigs tights and shoes as the Management desires.

MR. AND MRS. LEVY agree to pay all train and boat fares (3rd class only) after commencement of tour until termination of engagement.

This Agreement being made subject to the following rules, regulations and conditions :

LIST OF RULES.

1. **No Play, no Pay.**

2. Any Artiste or Artistes proving incompetent shall be liable to instant dismissal.

3. If any Artiste so far forgets his or her duty to the Manager and the Public as to be intoxicated in business, the Management shall have the right of instantly dismissing, without notice, anyone so offending, and shall not be liable for any Salary whatever, all claims for same being considered forfieted.

4. Every Member of the Company is expected to travel with the Company, or failing to do so, must pay his or her own fare.

5. No Member of the Company is allowed to act, sing, or appear publicly at any other theatre or place of entertainment without permission of the Management, specially obtained, in writing, in each separate instance. A breach of this article renders the Member liable to dismissal.

6. No Member of the Company is permitted to go in front of the house without the permission of the Management, the penalty being forfeiture of a night's salary.

7. Addressing the audience, without the permission from the Management, subjects the offender to immediate dismissal.

The contract for one of Stan's first professional engagements, "Sleeping Beauty," at a salary of £1 and 5 shillings.

In apparent emulation of one of his idols, Nat Wills, vaudeville's "Happy Tramp."

Stan (right) and Arthur Dandoe as the Barto Bros., 1912.

Ridiculous   Romans

— and —

Grotesque Gladiators

THE ...

BARTO BROS.

("Barmicuss" & "Sillicuss")

"The Rum 'uns from Rome"

In an Original Broad Burlesque Absurdity,

Introducing—

"BRUTUS"

The Only Filleted Horse
in Existence.

"TITUS"

The Famous Banana-
Eating Lion.

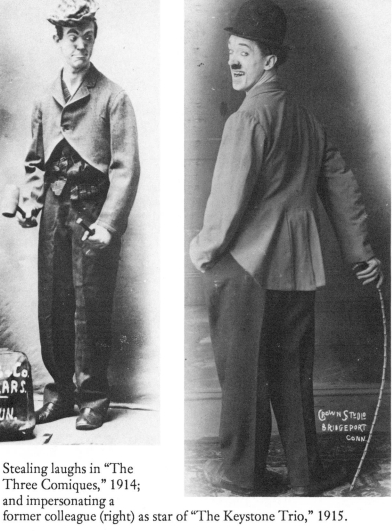

Stealing laughs in "The
Three Comiques," 1914;
and impersonating a
former colleague (right) as star of "The Keystone Trio," 1915.

had asked for originally. It was during this tour that Chaplin was signed by Mack Sennett to make films, thus permitting Stan to play the lead comedy roles in the company. But trouble impended at Philadelphia where Karno had signed a twelve-week contract with the Nixon-Nirdlinger circuit.

Stan:

"In this contract it was understood that Chaplin was to appear in the shows, but even though Chaplin had left the company for picture work, the company proceeded to Philadelphia, our manager informing the Nixon-Nirdlinger people that Chaplin wasn't with the company any more but also advising them that I was equally as good as Chaplin. They didn't agree to this arrangement. It was then suggested by our company manager that if they let us play one week with me in the part and if they weren't satisfied, they could cancel the balance of the contract. This wasn't agreed to either: they wanted Chaplin. It ended up, however, with their agreeing to accept the contract if Karno would bring over from England the principal comedian from the London Karno company named Dan Raynor. We laid off three weeks waiting for him. He came, we opened but the show was a flop, and after we played a couple weeks, the contract was canceled and the troupe disbanded. We got what work we could as individuals. I remember getting a day's work at a vaudeville house doing a shadowgraph act called *Evolution of Fashion,* about a drunk in a cafe. It was almost like a movie —acting in shadow pantomime before a white screen. As to the disbanded Karno troupe, those who wanted to return to England were given tickets, while those who didn't want to go could stay here. A fellow in the act and his wife, Mr. and Mrs. Edgar Hurley and I, decided to remain in this country and produce an act of our own. We proceeded to Chicago figuring to try out an act there and try it in and around the Midwest, planning if it was a success to bring it to New York. I wrote this act which I called *The Nutty Burglars*. We produced it in Chicago and played there and around there for several months."

The Nutty Burglars was a slight piece. The title characters are two noisy types who enter an apartment with larcenous intent. During their assault on a corner safe they are interrupted by a piquant maid. They immediately pose as icemen and she accepts the explanation. One of the burglars flirts heavily with her which allows his confederate to continue with the burgling. This thief lights the fuse on a hand bomb to blow the safe open. The climax of the act is the hasty passing of the sputtering bomb from one burglar to another before it is hastily thrown out the window. Explosion off—and a cop enters in black-powdered rags to arrest them. Stan described the act as "But no plot, just gags, anything for laughs." Despite its slightness, the act was taken under contract by a particularly astute booking agent, Gordon Bostock, who enhanced its playability considerably.

Stan:

"Bostock dressed it up, making it big time. He rehearsed the act personally and changed its name, calling it *The Keystone Trio*. He had me discard the character I was portraying and made me play it in the tramp character of Charlie Chaplin, just then becoming very popular in the Keystone Comedies. He also had Mr. and Mrs. Hurley change their characters to Chester Conklin and Mabel Normand, also great stars at Keystone, hence our being known as *The Keystone Trio*. The act proved to be a terrific hit. Since Chaplin and I both had the same kind of strong pantomime training, I could do his tramp just as he did it. The act and material remained just as I had written it, but with the new characterizations there was an added novelty touch which sent it over with a bang. Then differences arose between Hurley and me which caused a split. Hurley wanted to play the tramp role and he simply wasn't qualified to do so. Hurley quickly copyrighted the act, not telling me about it, claiming it as his material as a means to stop me from doing the act with another couple. He replaced me in the act with another fellow, Ted Banks. Then the theatre managers discovered I was not in the act, and it had become an inferior act anyway. They couldn't get further bookings and *The Keystone Trio* folded forever. It was then I produced a three-person act known as *The Stan Jefferson Trio*."

At which point, one is delighted to allow a gracious and spunky lady, still ebullient in her late eighties, to tell the story of her meeting Stan as well as something of the history of *The Stan Jefferson Trio*. Presently a Hollywood resident, Alice Cooke has vivid memories of her days with Stan. *

Alice Cooke:

"He was a delight. That's the only word I can use about him. He was the most generous and thoughtful man I have

---

*Alice Cooke died June 6, 1985.

ever known in my entire life—a long one. At the time I met him, I was half of the double act, Cooke and Hamilton. My husband was Baldwin Cooke, or Baldy as everyone used to call him. Well, Baldy and I were playing our act in 1915 in St. Thomas, Ontario, when we first met Stan. We played on the same bill with Stan and the Hurleys when they were doing *The Keystone Trio* act, and Baldy and I became close friends with Stan right away. Then a few months later, Stan split with the Hurleys, and so we all got together to do our own three-act. This was *The Stan Jefferson Trio,* named after Stan, of course. I think we were the three happiest people in the world, doing that act. When Stan first thought of the idea, he said he hadn't had a vacation since he was a little boy and he wanted one. So he had the idea for us to rent a cottage at some beach where we could go swimming and that's where he would write an act for us. We would rehearse every day as well as having a good time, and we'd get that act ready for a fall showing. This was June 1916.

"We rented a darling cottage near the Atlantic Highlands in New Jersey. Stan wrote an act which he called *The Crazy Cracksman,* and we rehearsed hard every day and had it ready for our fall showing which Claude Bostock, brother of Gordon, Stan's old agent, got for us."

The Crazy Cracksman, in Stan's words many years later, was "not the greatest act in the world but it was fun—and anyway, anything for a living!" Alice Cooke played an actress, Baldy was her English dude press agent. The actress complains that she has had very little publicity lately, and the agent promptly suggests they hire someone to steal her jewels, thereby securing front page attention. Baldy leaves to hire an actor to do the job. Alice takes up her knitting and rocks away contentedly. Enter a real burglar, attired as Charlie Chaplin's tramp, played by Stan. Stan, whose costume is hung with kitchen utensils of all kinds, is taken aback by seeing the lady, but espying a piano, quickly passes himself off as a piano tuner. The lady takes him to be the hired burglar and addresses him familiarly as such. Physical gags abound: Stan does classic pratfalls, sits on flypaper which he disengages extravagantly, is liberally sprayed with seltzer water, and the like. Shortly after, enter another burglar, not a hired article, but Baldy in thief's disguise. He has been unable to hire a man and has taken on the job himself. His sneaky entrance through the window, however, has aroused the suspicions of a cop who follows him in, and arrests both him and the original burglar who is recognized as an escaped felon. The cop (usually played by a local stage manager) hauls them both protestingly away as Alice placidly resumes her knitting. As to the deep comedy values of this sketch, Stan would say smilingly in later years, "You honest to God had to be there."

Alice Cooke:

"Well, sir, the act was a riot, and why wouldn't it be with Stan doing all those crazily wonderful gags. One I remember in particular. He got up on a pretty high ladder and purposely fell all the way down it, slipping and sliding with arms and feet all akimbo. It looked so dangerous a fall— and it could have been if he didn't do it just right—but at the same time it was the funniest thing you ever saw. In our act we had lots and lots of props, things we used to get laughs with, and we always had to send on to the theatre where we were booked a list of the props that we would need. In this way, the property man at that theatre (and every vaudeville theatre had such a man) would have the props ready for us by the time we got there.

"Now, we had a prop list which was at least a couple of pages long—fancy furniture, ladder, a safe to break into, et cetera. Usually as soon as we'd get to the theatre, the prop man would greet us and he'd frown. We got no welcome from *him*. On one occasion the prop man said that our list was unlike any list he had ever gotten in all his life. He said he'd never gotten a list like that ever. Well, said Stan and Baldy, you just got one from us. And the prop man said, 'Do you *need* all this stuff?' Stan said, 'Yes, we need it.' The man said, 'Do you really need it *all?*' Same answer from Stan. Finally after the man read through the list to the very end just shaking his head in disbelief, Stan said, 'You know, we can go out and do our act on a bare stage, but all those props make our act what it *should be*. And they help make it *good*. But we don't absolutely deep down have to have them, no.' So that prop man walked away, and when we came to the theatre that night, he had every *one* of those props for us, all ready! That prop man was a man who appreciated an act that wanted to do its very best and worked hard at it. But he was just one man. Most of the other prop men really kicked. Stan and Baldy, instead of bawling out prop men when they objected to our list, just took it in their stride, kidded the prop men and said, 'Don't worry, we'll get along.' And so we didn't play *once* but what we didn't have all the props we needed. It was Stan and Baldy's attitude that made it possible. They didn't argue or demand to see the manager, as they could have done. They were warm and pleasant to everybody, and I can tell you it was wonderful working with those two wonderful men.

"Anyway, as I said, our act was a great success and our agent, Claude Bostock, was able to get us a long route, starting on the Proctor time. We were billed as *The Stan Jefferson Trio* in *The Crazy Cracksman,* and oh, my, didn't we have fun! We didn't have ambitions to go on to bigger things. Not us, not Stan either. In those days vaudevillians just lived for fun. That's all we thought of. We lived for fun, food, drinks, and good times. So, Stan was always a happy-go-lucky. He used to tell us funny things about what happened when he first came to the States with Karno in 1910. But nobody had any happier times than we did with *The Stan Jefferson Trio* for two wonderful seasons. We got $175 a week for our act, which wasn't bad money, and we split it three ways.

"You could do a lot with $175 a week in those days, and we did it! We just spent it all (it seemed) when we got it, not giving a thought for the next day or week. I remember once when we were playing Troy, New York, on the Proctor time. As I said, being young, we always spent our salary when we got it, and when we were in Troy we used to go to this nice place, The Hofbrau, and spend it. This one night we were very, very short—it was the night before we got our salary, and so we pooled our money to see if we had enough. We found we had funds enough for each of us to have a ham sandwich and two glasses of beer, and plus even a small tip for the waiter. The Hofbrau was a beautiful place, a great white marble floor, and we were sitting at our table, just having ordered, when an English friend of Stan's who was playing the Keith house in town came in. He saw Stan. Stan hailed him over, and being the great sport and trouper he was, Stan asked the fellow, 'What'll you have to eat? What'll you have with us?'—absolutely forgetting that we didn't have the money to pay for it. So this fellow immediately ordered a club sandwich and a highball!

"So, with that, Baldy and Stan both realized that we didn't have the money, and across the table they made faces at each other, wondering what on earth they were going to do. Then I happened to remember that in my purse I had one of those dime banks that has to have five dollars in it before the thing will open. And I knew there wasn't five dollars in there, but still there was *something*—so I nudged my husband, and passed him the bank. So right away he winked to Stan that it was all right and not to worry. So my husband struggled with that thing, trying to be unobtrusive with it. He took a fork and picked at it under the table, and he finally succeeded with it but he pulled too hard and suddenly all those dimes —$4 worth—sprayed out and flew everywhere all over that white marble floor, under just everybody's table, and Stan and Baldy got up and crawled on their hands and knees under all the tables near us to get those dimes! Stan never got tired of telling that story. Oh, the fun we had in those days!

"When we first teamed up with Stan, I honestly didn't know if it would be a good thing for me personally because my husband and I had always worked alone, and we were very devoted and went everywhere together—and I thought with the extra man coming in, it's two men together in a sense, and I'd be somewhat left out. But never—right from the beginning—never did that happen. The boys used to go down to the agent's to book our act, and when they got through, they'd go over to a place on Broadway and 43rd, Dowling's, for a drink. And my husband never failed to call and tell me to come down and join them for a drink. And that's the way the three of us were always. Just three pals— I was left out of nothing. Those happy days just seemed as if they would never end."

But they did, because of the appearance on the scene of a young lady from Australia named Mae Charlotte Dahlberg. Born in Australia on May 24, 1888, this vivacious singer and dancer was doing a dancing sister act in vaudeville with Cissy Hayden under the billing of *The Hayden Sisters* in the years just prior to and during World War I. The Hayden act and Stan's act were on the same bill in a small Pennsylvania town in 1918 when Stan and Mae, in Alice Cooke's words, "hit it off right away." A few weeks later, Stan sadly told the Hamiltons that he wanted to leave their three-act but suggested as replacement an old friend of his from the Karno company, Billy Crackles. The Hamiltons were upset by Stan's departure but resolving to make the best of it took the act out again with the new partner. Their new partner's close friendship with the bottle forced them back into their old double act. They felt certain that they would never see Stan again.

Stan entered into a very active partnership with Mae Dahlberg. Mae had as vigorous a sense of humor as Stan's, and it is likely (or so said Mae in later years) that she would have married Stan were it not that she already had a husband in Australia, a gentleman not interested in divorce. With *The Crazy Cracksman* in the purview of the Hamiltons, Stan was faced with the need to write an act for himself and Mae. What he came up with was an act for two female comics—Mae and Stan in old biddy guise. George Burns, who in those days was teamed with Billy Loraine, remembers this act as ". . . a kind of a sketch act, with Stan in drag —very ratty and funny—possibly playing his wife's mother. He cried a lot in the act and got pushed around, taking many comedy falls."

It was at this time, in his first days with Mae, that Stan Laurel received his name. It is a particular joy of this biographer that I finally resolved the mystery—for so it has been for many years—of the origin of the name "Laurel." In 1953 when I first asked Stan how the name came to him, he honestly could not remember. He had a vague idea that it happened in 1918, and he also remembered that his impelling reason to seek a new name was superstition. "Stan Jefferson" is thirteen letters, and like many show business people, he did not relish flying in the face of good luck by advertising bad luck, as he so considered his old billing after a bit. The name "Laurel" came to him from Mae Dahlberg, a matter I learned from the lady herself, the lady who for many years following Stan's ascendancy to fame proclaimed herself his common-law wife, and who in many ways, was.

I interviewed Mae Laurel a year before her death in 1969 at the Sayville Nursing Home, Sayville, New York. Frail, looking very withdrawn from the world's troubles, this pleasant-mannered old lady listened to my many questions about Stan with unmarred patience. Some details of their many experiences during those years she could recall only vaguely. But on one matter, she had total recall.

Mae Laurel:

"I can remember just how Stan got the name Laurel. It was not long after we were teamed together, and we were traveling as a double act sometimes called Stan and Mae Jefferson, or mostly Stan Jefferson, with me as assistant. Stan had been thinking for some time that Stan Jefferson had thirteen letters in it, and it began to prey on his mind a bit. He said we should be looking for a new name. Well, one night after the show, I was in the dressing room at whatever theatre we were playing, looking at an old history book that someone in the previous week's show must have left there in one corner of the dressing table. I opened it up casual like, and I came to an etching or a drawing of a famous old Roman general. Scipio Africanus Major. I'll never forget that name. Around his head he wore a laurel, a wreath of laurel. I learned later that laurel leaves are really bay leaves. Anyway, I looked at that headpiece of laurel, and that word stayed with me. I said it aloud, 'Laurel. Laurel. Stan Laurel.' Stan looked up from what he was doing and he said, 'What?' I said, Laurel. Stan Laurel. How about that for a name?' He repeated it aloud, too. 'Stan Laurel. Sounds very good.' That's how he got his name. It was that simple."

The act became Stan and Mae Laurel, a length easy for marquee billing and euphonious into the bargain. This was the only harmony in the act. Almost from the beginning of their association which lasted off and on almost a decade, Stan and Mae argued bitterly yet somehow felt a deep mutual attraction. "Whenever I played with them on the same bill on the Pantages circuit," George Burns remembers, "the Laurels seemed to be fighting day and night. And with the thin-walled dressing rooms on that circuit, they could easily be heard all over the theatre. But then—when the dressing room door would open, there they'd both be—smiling at each other as if nothing were going on. Then the minute the door was closed, the battle would start again. She had the voice, he had the talent."

Not long after Stan and Mae became an act, they were booked into the Hippodrome Theatre, Los Angeles, owned by Adolph Ramish, an unpretentious man with a gift for comedy appraisal. He was the first man in Stan's life to realize the cinematic potential of this pleasantly handsome young vaudevillian with an unerring sense of the ridiculous. Ramish furnished the money to make a pilot film for display of the Laurel comic wares to potential bookers. Ramish asked Bobby Williamson, a comedian and director from

Florida's Kalem Studios, to fit up a story for Stan. Bobby and Stan constructed a mildly funny story about a lunatic who escapes from an institution wearing an ordinary business suit and a Napoleon hat. This 1917 film, *Nuts in May*, seems to have disappeared but Stan never considered it much of a loss. The film was previewed at the Hippodrome and in the audience that night were Charlie Chaplin and the head of Universal Studios, Carl Laemmle. They had a delightful time and for a few weeks Chaplin was interested in Stan as a possible member of the Chaplin company. But he did not follow through, and Carl Laemmle signed Stan to a one-year contract with Universal.

In 1917 Stan commenced a series of pictures for Universal using the soubriquet, Hickory Hiram. "I made only three or four of them," Stan remembered, "and there was some jealousy on the lot from other comedians because I was a newcomer who might possibly be cutting in on their livelihood. In any case, the films were pretty bad, and were released, so I understand, to all the very best comfort stations. At this time Laemmle was going through reorganization problems and all contracts were canceled."

Mae Laurel insisted, and she was very good at insistence, on being in the Hickory Hiram films. It was at this time that Stan and Mae met an athletic young man, Joe Rock, who had recently come to Hollywood after working as a stunt man for Vitagraph Studios in Brooklyn. Rock became a featured player in two-reel comedies. In a few years, Rock was to play a vital part in structuring Stan's career but in 1917 as a comedy star in his own right, Rock was concerned with extending his own work. He recognized that Stan might contribute to the Rock films a vital talent but Rock also saw this unique ability being sandbagged. *

Joe Rock:

"Those early films of Stan, the Hickory Hiram two-reelers, were to some degree always spoiled by Mae's appearance in them. She was Stan's partner so Stan faithfully insisted that she be in them. It was a mistake. Mae was older than Stan, or at least looked a lot older. In any case, she wasn't photogenic. She never photographed like an ingenue should; she looked more like a character actress, even if not made up as one. In their vaudeville act, which was a knockabout, slapstick dancing and singing act, they were fine—and could get bookings on any top circuit. But Stan grew sick of the constant battles he had with Mae and he was determined to break up the association. He knew that going out with the vaudeville act would only prolong his being with her, and so he wanted to stay in Hollywood and make pictures.

"The only trouble was that after he made those Hickory Hiram things with Mae in them, no comedy producer worthy of the name would have anything to do with Mae, as Mae kept insisting that she had to be in Stan's pictures. He was just too softhearted to tell her to get out of his life. In those Hickory Hiram pictures, Mae was just plain vulgar. In nearly every film she was in, there'd be one or more scenes where she and Stan would both be going over a wall or through a high open window or through a transom over a door, and Mae would be the first to go. Stan would be

*Joe Rock died December 5, 1984.

trying to push her up and over, struggling to do it. Stan's final push would consist of his hand going under her dress, pushing her on the fanny. Mae loved this gag (if you can call it that). She would act like someone getting goosed, turning her face toward the camera and reacting violently. This was good for laughs but it brought the censors down on both distributors and theatre owners. Having Mae as a partner limited Stan a great deal, and Stan's writers and gag men in those early pictures always felt limited in their work because of her. They hated to write for Mae. I didn't like him to work with me for that reason."

The disinclination of distributors to take the Hickory Hiram product and Universal Pictures' reorganization sent the Laurel act back into vaudeville. Stan returned occasionally during 1918 to make five one-reelers, totally innocuous films, for Hal Roach, a man Stan met that year, and who had enjoyed the Laurel antics on the vaudeville stage. "Those first Roach films had no particular plots," Stan said. "Just a funny situation—like a man working as a short order cook in a diner—and working in all the gags you could."

Also in 1918, Stan's vaudeville act was scouted by G. M. "Broncho Billy" Anderson, Hollywood's first cowboy star, who as a producer began to foresee much profit in the comedy film. Anderson asked Stan to do a two-reel pilot film which would serve as Anderson's calling card to New York bankers and investors. The film, *Lucky Dog*, directed by Jesse Robbins, is mildly amusing for all its slight plot: Stan finds a stray dog and enters it in a dog show, wins first prize, the owners appear and he is accused of dognapping. He is forgiven. Insubstantial stuff indeed, but it has one moment charged with excitement for comedy film buffs today. As Stan hurries down a street, he is held up briefly by a masked bandit—a bulky man who succeeds admirably in conveying oppressive comic menace.

This was Oliver "Babe" Hardy, a twenty-five-year-old Georgia-born actor, lately come to California from Florida and New York where he had been playing "heavies" in Billy West Comedies. During the making of *Lucky Dog*, Stan Laurel and Oliver Hardy were, in Stan's words ". . . friendly, but there was nothing about the picture or our own personal relationship to suggest that we might ever become partners. He and I were just two working comics, glad to have a job—any job." Babe Hardy (in subsequent pages, Hardy offscreen is Babe, Hardy onscreen is Ollie) was an adept at scene stealing even at this early date, and Stan was not sorry that the Hardy role was brief. Shortly after the film was made, Stan went back to vaudeville.

In 1919 Stan returned from tour briefly to work at Vitagraph Pictures with Larry Semon, then a reigning comedy star. The diminutive Semon, a former newspaper cartoonist, was a man with high regard for a gag and with a deep, abiding suspicion of supporting players with talents equal to his. Because Stan ostentatiously fell into this category, he was consigned once more to vaudeville and its grueling rigors. The peripatetic nature of the vaudevillian's life is vividly illustrated in this listing of the playing dates for Stan and Mae Laurel across three of their busiest years as a team. Inclusive playing dates are shown. Bookings marked with an asterisk

An ad for Stan's second film, "released at all the first-run comfort stations." 1918.

Oliver "Babe" Hardy and another future partner — Lois Neilson, destined to become Laurel's first wife — with Billy West in a 1918 King-Bee comedy.

The short-lived team of Larry Semon and Stan Laurel in a 1918 Vitagraph two-reeler.

Stan and Babe, paired by coincidence, circa 1918-19.

Posing with Mae Charlotte Dahlberg, who toured the Pantages circuit with him from 1918-21.

indicate the publication date of that issue of *Billboard* magazine which reports the act as playing or shortly to play that
theatre.

APPEARANCE
DATE   THEATRE AND CITY

1918

*October 12**	PRINCESS, Wichita, Kansas
*November 16**	MAJESTIC, Springfield, Illinois
*November 23**	BIJOU, Battle Creek, Michigan
*November 30**	BIJOU, Lansing, Michigan
December 2–7	PALACE, Flint, Michigan
*December 7**	BIJOU, Bay City, Michigan
*December 21**	ORPHEUM, South Bend, Indiana

1919

*January 18**	ORPHEUM, Champaign, Illinois
*January 25**	ORPHEUM, Peoria, Illinois
*February 1**	HIPPODROME, Terre Haute, Indiana
*February 22**	PALACE, Moline, Illinois
*March 8**	COLUMBIA, Davenport, Iowa
March 10–12	ORPHEUM, Sioux City, Iowa
*March 22**	EMPRESS, Omaha, Nebraska
*April 5**	NEW PALACE, St. Paul, Minnesota
April 7–9	NEW GRAND, Duluth, Minnesota
*April 12**	NEW PALACE, Superior, Wisconsin
*April 19**	ORPHEUM, Green Bay, Wisconsin
*May 10**	FAMILY, Lafayette, Indiana
*May 17**	COLONIAL, Logansport, Indiana
*June 7**	STRAND, Owosso, Michigan
*June 14**	BRANT, Brantford, Ontario
June 16–18	GRAND OPERA HOUSE, Peterboro, Ontario
*June 21**	GRAND OPERA HOUSE, Kingston, Ontario
*July 5**	YONGE, Toronto, Ontario

July 19*	RIALTO, Chicago, Illinois
August 16*	PANTAGES, Winnipeg, Manitoba
August 18–20	PANTAGES, Saskatoon, Saskatchewan
August 25–30	PANTAGES, Edmonton, Alberta
September 1–6	PANTAGES, Calgary, Alberta
September 8–10	PANTAGES, Great Falls, Montana
September 13*	PANTAGES, Helena, Montana
September 15–17	PANTAGES, Butte, Montana
September 20*	PANTAGES, Missoula, Montana
September 22–27	PANTAGES, Spokane, Washington
September 29–	PANTAGES, Seattle, Washington
October 4	
October 6–11	PANTAGES, Vancouver, British Columbia
October 13–18	PANTAGES, Victoria, British Columbia
October 20–25	PANTAGES, Tacoma, Washington
October 27–	
November 1	PANTAGES, Portland, Oregon
November 1*	PANTAGES, San Francisco, California
November 10–15	PANTAGES, Oakland, California
November 17–29	PANTAGES, Los Angeles, California
November 29*	PANTAGES, Salt Lake City, Utah
December 1–6	PANTAGES, Ogden, Utah
December 6*	PANTAGES, San Diego, California
December 8–13	PANTAGES, Long Beach, California
December 15–20	PANTAGES, Salt Lake City, Utah
December 27*	PANTAGES, Ogden, Utah
December 29–	
January 3	PANTAGES, Denver, Colorado

1920

January 17*	ORPHEUM, Waco, Texas
January 19–24	ROYAL, San Antonio, Texas
January 31*	WICHITA, Wichita Falls, Texas
February 2–7	JEFFERSON, Dallas, Texas

February 28*	FULTON, Brooklyn, New York
March 6*	DELANCEY STREET, New York City
March 27*	LOEW'S, London, Ontario
April 10*	YONGE, Toronto, Ontario
April 17*	LOEW'S, Hamilton, Ontario
April 24*	BOULEVARD, New York City
May 1*	LINCOLN SQUARE, New York City
May 8*	METROPOLITAN, Brooklyn
May 15*	DELANCEY STREET, New York City
May 22*	EMPIRE, Fall River, Massachusetts
May 29*	BROADWAY, Springfield, Massachusetts
June 5*	VICTORIA, New York City
June 12*	LINCOLN SQUARE, New York City
August 28*	PALACE, Hartford, Connecticut
September 4*	POLI, Bridgeport, Connecticut
September 11	POLI, Scranton, Pennsylvania

A fatiguing schedule in a day when traveling was not easy, and this was a schedule maintained unrelentingly (except for a few months off to make films) well into the 1920s.

In 1922, "Broncho Billy" Anderson, armed with a copy of *Lucky Dog*, had made adequate inroads on investor sources to find the backing for other Laurel films. Anderson produced for Stan a number of extremely clever two-reel parodies of then currently successful feature films, among them and typically *Mud and Sand*, a spoof of Rudolph Valentino's *Blood and Sand* which featured Stan as that immortal lover, Rhubarb Vaselino. Anderson also did a take-off on Douglas Fairbanks's Robin Hood entitled *When Knights Were Cold*, which contained according to Stan ". . . one beautifully funny sequence that I've never seen in movies, either before

33

or since. We had an army of knights in a chase sequence. There were over three hundred of them working with basket horses . . . the circus-clown type horses, with the men's legs extending beneath the little papier-mâché horses built around them. It was hilarious, like some of those circus routines."

A few months before he died in 1971, I interviewed "Broncho Billy." A patient in the Motion Picture Country House, Woodland Hills, California, he looked back over a lifetime of service to the movies with vast affection for all those years and for most of the people he knew. He had particular love for Stan. "Stan was a wonderful fellow—so cheerful around the lot," said Billy. "He just made you feel good the minute he walked in. Not only that, but he was always very much concerned with making the picture a success even if it meant working extra-long hours and doing things that weren't easy. Not a complaint from Stan, ever. We made some awfully good pictures, and I think we could have made even better pictures—but we just didn't have enough money in return bookings to make the ones we wanted to make, so Stan just had to go back into vaudeville."

In 1923, Stan was called back from the road to make a series of one- and two-reel comedies for Hal Roach. He did these for Roach with considerable pleasure because it meant a certain amount of relief from the nagging of his partner. Mae's shrewish nature was never far from the surface but it seemed to manifest itself most assertively when they were by themselves on tour. In the film studio she had less opportunity to dominate.

The 1923–24 Roach series introduced Stan to a man who

was going to be a comic foil of his for decades to come. This was splendidly beetle-browed James Finlayson who was to remain Stan's friend and co-worker until Finlayson's death in 1953. Representative of the early Roach films they did together is a one-reeler, *Near Dublin,* released in May 1924, which still exhibits fulsome comic gusto when viewed today. It is a period piece, set in the late eighteenth century.

Near Dublin is a small rural village named Trenchcoat where mayhem is the operative way of life. The focus of much of this distemper is the town bad guy, Finlayson, "Fin" as he was called on and off the set. "Fin" is the owner of Trenchcoat's only brickyard and a perpetual, glowering squint. His uningratiating personality makes him a frequent recipient of his product—usually on the back of his head. As the film begins, "Fin" demonstrates his typical warmth of personality by kicking a little boy who has been playing with some "Fin" bricks. In shining contrast to "Fin" is Stan, our hero—"so bright," a title tells us, "that he practically glows in the dark." He is the postman, neatly but rakishly attired as the conventional stage Irishman, sucking on a pipe with inverted bowl. On this day his first delivery is of a lively pig, which has set its wits against Stan's. This is pretty much of an even match. The pig escapes from Stan's grasp and scampers around the corner. Stan literally throws himself around that corner and collides with "Fin" who is chasing the little boy he kicked earlier. The boy finds a remarkably convenient fat tomato and its succulence leaves its mark on "Fin." Stan laughs gleefully and departs.

Cut to the home of the heroine. "Fin" is presenting the

girl and her father with the rent bill. Unless it is paid, they must vacate the house forthwith. "Fin," in traditional "me proud beauty" stance offers himself as a substitute for the rent but Stan comes in—with a roll of bills, and gives two of them to the delighted father for costs in hand. Before Stan can put the rest of the roll back in his pocket, Papa very calmly grabs it and gives the roll to "Fin" for added payment. Then Papa cunningly engages "Fin" in argument and picks his pocket of all the money. Stan looks on approvingly and after "Fin's" departure holds out his hand to receive his money. Papa looks blankly at Stan's hand, smiles, and shakes it vigorously. Stan registers shocked disapproval into the camera but turns to the girl with a Chaplinesque hunch of the shoulders as if to say, "Oh, well!" and kisses her.

Cut to Trenchcoat's annual gala—where everyone carries bricks to guard against bad luck. Jolly games proliferate and in one of them a blindfolded Stan is positioned to locate and bite into an apple swinging at the end of a string. A helpful friend places Stan, then substitutes a brick for the apple and pulling it back lets it swing smack into Stan's nose. (The gags in *Near Dublin* strive to avoid subtlety.) Stan is understandably stunned at this jape, flexes his face strongly to recover and after removing the blindfold seems to accept it all in a spirit of good fun. He points to the brick smilingly, as if it were an object of whimsy, a token of good-spirited fun.

Then in a close-up, an aside to the audience, he scowls, reaches back into his postal sack for a brick, and again smiling turns to face his jokester crony. This worthy has been enjoying his little prank with the others, and as he looks away for a moment, Stan cleans off the brick with his sleeve, kisses it and beams glowingly at the jokester. As the jokester turns to face him, Stan swings the brick from where he has been hiding it behind his back and heaves it directly into the jokester's mouth. Stan then randomly swats a few more people with his brick and a jolly donnybrook ensues.

In this scene, Stan shows an astonishing array of facial expressions. In quick turn he is jubilantly playful, stunned, grindingly bellicose, recuperative, jovially forgiving, and cunningly vindictive. His eyebrows are wildly mobile and serve as the petard for these constantly changing expressions. This countenance is the polar opposite of his later slow-reflexed dimwit face during the Hardy partnership. This is Laurel à la Chaplin.

After the brick-tossing melee is terminated by the police (urged on by "Fin"), Stan is hauled away to jail but not before he has liberally showered his captors with bricks, too. In Trenchcoat Municipal Prison, Stan engineers his escape by crawling over the cellar floor as if searching for something. The intensity of his hunt leads the guard to get down on his hands and knees to join Stan in the search, and as he does, Stan very calmly crawls right out of the door to freedom. Once free, Stan runs to his girl, finds her still menaced by "Fin's" attentions. The two men fight and Stan plays dead in order to pull a rather ghostly trick. "Fin" is arrested for the "death" and is tried for murder in a barn. During these proceedings Stan appears atop a hayloft in ghost-like stance and make-up. Fear and pandemonium. This macabre little episode slaking his thirst for revenge, he embraces the heroine and all is well. Fadeout.

For those who might wonder at the galloping pace of these events and the almost studied lack of logic and rational motivation for the film's action, it must be remembered that this is a one-reel film, running approximately ten minutes, and comedy makers in 1924 felt obliged to give the customer as much action as possible within that time. The rubric of early film farce was "The most, done by the quickest, at the fastest." It was a pace which Laurel and Hardy were deliberately to reverse.

In *Near Dublin* as in all the Roach one-reelers made at the time, Stan was given the normal love interest, a pretty and vivacious ingenue, who added tasty seasoning to the film. The presence of these young women in the films drove Mae Laurel to bursts of vituperation.

Joe Rock:

"Mae refused to admit that she was not an ingenue. Actually, she would have done very well as a character woman, both in comedies and dramatic features, but she wouldn't have it. I guess she never looked in a mirror. She wanted to be teamed as Stan's girl friend and none of the studios could ever agree to that. So, frequently, Stan would try to team them anyway, knowing that if he didn't there'd be a battle royal when he got home. But things got tougher and tougher for him. Jobs got scarcer because the studios just didn't want Mae. At this time Stan's closest friend was a director named Perce Pembroke who had worked for me various times.

Perce had also directed Stan in his 'Broncho Billy' series. Perce came to me and said Stan's financial position was very bad and would I be willing to hire Stan? I said I'd meet with Stan but I insisted that Mae not come with him.

"When Stan came, I explained that because I didn't know whether or not I would be able to sell a comedy series with him, I would be willing to advance him some money to live, to get some new clothes, et cetera, and I would go East and sound out the distributors on their perhaps buying a Stan Laurel series. I told Stan I would not risk my money however if he insisted on having Mae in the films. He agreed with me, saying he understood the situation. He actually had patches in the seat of his pants and when he stood up, he pulled his coat tail down to cover them. He had cardboard in his shoes to cover the holes in them, and he admitted that he had never been lower in his life. I gave him $1,000 and then I left for New York.

"In New York I tried to persuade the distributors that Stan was a changed man, that I was giving him a good salary and a percentage of the profits, and that in view of our long friendship he would come through for me. I knew *they* knew that probably because of Mae, Stan once had a little liquor problem, but I explained that this never existed when Stan was working at something he loved. But the distributors wouldn't take a chance on signing a contract to book my projected twelve Stan Laurel pictures for the coming year because they thought Stan just wouldn't come through for me. They warned me.

"I ignored their warning and went back to make the pictures. The first picture, and much depended on it, was *Detained,* which we projected to make in September 1924. Stan helped our writers prepare it, sets were built (at Universal Studios), actors and actresses were hired, costumes fitted—and the date was set for the first day of shooting.

"One day before shooting started, Stan came into my office, and although he stayed near the door I could see three or four deep, vivid scratches on the left side of his face from under the ear, right across his face and mouth. I was shocked beyond belief. Stan said, 'You won't believe it, but I was playing with our cat, and I held her too tight when she pulled away from me—and she scratched me.' I looked at him for a minute and then I said, 'What's your cat's name— Mae?'

"He tried to convince me his story was true, and it took a good many minutes before he admitted what I suspected. He then said that Mae wanted to know what costume she was wearing in the picture. I said, 'What picture?' Stan replied, 'Mae convinced me after nearly an all-night argument that we must continue to work together, so she is ready to come over to be fitted for her costume so she'll be ready to shoot tomorrow.' I said, 'Stan, you know me better than to think I'm stupid enough to allow Mae or even you to run my business! We have a contract which was approved by both of you and we've been at least three weeks preparing the story, building the sets, hiring our people and never was there any mention or *need* to mention Mae being in the picture. Now you spring this on me a day before shooting starts!'

"Stan said, 'You can't let all that money go to waste, and if Mae can't work in the film, I won't either.' I pointed out that I could call half a dozen comedians who could be ready to take his place even though they might not be ready to start the next day, and that we could shoot around them until they could start.

"After about ten minutes, I could see Stan was losing his bravado, and I sensed he was hoping I could suggest something that would bail him out. I said I'd be happy to speak to Mae personally, and he was agreeable but didn't believe I'd be able to budge her. I phoned Mae and said, 'Mae, Stan tells me you don't have your wardrobe for tomorrow. Why don't you come right over and we'll talk about it?'

"In fifteen minutes she breezed into my office like Gloria Swanson in *Sunset Boulevard*. I asked her to sit down. (I was afraid she'd fall down when she got the bad news.) Stan was sitting nearby. I told her Stan said he wouldn't work unless she was in the picture and I asked her, 'Is that correct?' She said, 'Absolutely!' I said, 'What would you say, Mae, if I told you that if Stan won't work because you're not in the picture I'd just get myself another comedian to replace him?' 'You can't do that,' Mae said, 'Stan has a contract and the sets are built and the people are hired, and you *must* shoot with Stan!'

"I said very quietly, 'Mae, you have been a stone around Stan's neck for years. You say you love him but your actions now are keeping him from making a living for the both of you. I gave him money for food and the clothes you are wearing now, and you waited until you thought I wouldn't be able to get another comedian. Well, your little plan won't work.'

"She said very stubbornly, 'But what about Stan's contract?' I opened my desk drawer, drew out Stan's contract, and I said, 'Here is Stan's contract!' I then tore it in half and gave both pieces to Stan. I told him I was sorry it all turned out this way, I had thought surely we were going to have a nice association with each other because of our mutual respect for each other as evidenced by the $1,000 I had given him. But I added quickly, 'I don't want the money back. We'll charge it up to the production. But, honestly, Stan, I did think Mae loved you more than this.'

"Stan just sat there, not able to say a word. Mae sat there too in stunned silence, and then she began to cry. She did love him, she said—he'd be lost without her, he depended on her, they were good for each other—so forth and so on. I agreed that a professional break between them would be hard but it was necessary and after all they still had each other. She finally gave in and they both went away in better spirits than I had anticipated. We had to cover Stan's scratches with thin surgical tape and make-up."

With Stan secure, the Joe Rock producing organization went into high gear. In addition to the Stan Laurel comedies, Rock was making a series with Jimmy Aubrey, a versatile comedian and, like Stan, an alumnus of the Fred Karno troupe. There was one frightening moment for Joe Rock when, after making several Laurel and Aubrey comedies, the distributing organization appeared to be foundering financially. This was the Lewis J. Selznick group. Selznick, the father of David O. and Myron Selznick, had sent out across the country 1,050 prints of the seven Laurel and Aubrey comedies then made and was anticipating even wider distribution when the Selznick empire began to crumble. Rock rushed to New York and secretly obtained a court order just in time for the Laurel and Aubrey prints to be moved out of the Selznick exchanges and into the F.B.O. exchanges. Rock found new financing, and he returned to California in high spirits.

Joe Rock:

"Mae Laurel kept to her promise and never came to the studio. Stan was happy and worked on gags, stories, and so on, did his daily acting job, saw all the rushes and contributed his ideas to the cutting of the films. He never grumbled if we had to work late, and he was at the studio bright and early each morning. In this happy fashion, we made *Detained, Mandarin Mix-up, Monsieur Don't Care,* and *West of Hot Dog.*

"Then, during the making of a picture fittingly titled *Somewhere in Wrong,* things *began* to go wrong. Little by little, the atmosphere on the Stan Laurel Comedies production unit started to change. Stan began to be late most mornings. He looked tired, as if he was up late the night before. He wasn't the easygoing fellow so eager to make a good film. He started to become impatient with his fellow workers, which was so unlike him; he now resented having to reshoot scenes. This went on for a couple more pictures. I knew things must be getting out of hand because of Mae, and I finally got him to admit that this was true. He said Mae was unhappy because she wasn't working in the films with him.

"We were about to make a picture called *The Snow Hawk*, and since we were going away for a week or so on location to shoot it near Lake Arrowhead and Big Bear, Mae wanted to come along. By making Stan miserable and unhappy, she knew pressure could be brought on me to use her. When Stan finally begged me to allow her *just* to come on location with us, he promised she wouldn't visit any shooting locations but would confine herself to the village where we'd be living. Stan would have his own bungalow.

"We had, I imagine, over fifty people in our unit—actors, production staff, technicians—beside many residents of the area directly or indirectly working on the picture. Things had to be run very efficiently, like an army unit. Three or four people were put in each bungalow; we ate breakfast and dinner at the Main Lodge where our bulletin board was displayed with its vital regulations and schedules. Discipline was at the heart of everything we did. Stan had a bungalow with Mae, and I had one to myself. The second day of shooting my wife, Louise, came up to join me.

"The third day of shooting, I had to leave location (about twenty miles away from our living quarters) in order to get something at the Lodge. I did so and started back to location but my car, despite the chains I had on my tires, just wouldn't make it up a nearby hill going to location. I made a dozen runs, but no luck. So I returned to the village and there I ran into Mae who was just coming out of the Lodge. We spoke, and I told her about my trouble. We talked for about five minutes; she went to her bungalow, and I went to the Lodge. Now, Mae didn't know that my wife had come up to join me.

"The next day Stan took me aside and asked me point-blank if I had asked Mae to come to my bungalow the day before! She said I had told her Stan would be late coming back that day, and that I had always had a yen for her, and so on. I looked at Stan and asked him if he *really* believed that. He said he didn't know—she was so upset about it, because among other things I had kept a tight hold of her arm, frightening her to death.

"When I told Stan that Louise had come up earlier and had been at my bungalow all the day before, Stan didn't know what to say. He apologized for having believed Mae's story, and he admitted Mae had pulled this same stunt before, at other studios. The truth is, Mae wanted Stan to go back into vaudeville with her but realized he wouldn't leave Hollywood now—and so she was fed up with America. Stan said that if she had enough money to leave, she'd go back to Australia. Stan was all for this idea although he couldn't let her think he did, of course. Mae had come to this country in the days before passports but at the time I'm speaking of, 1925, she might have some difficulties getting back.

"So I called up a friend of mine in the British Consulate, a Mr. Johnson, and got things straightened out with him so that she could get back home without red tape. Mae was surprisingly agreeable and went down to the Consulate to fill out the forms. I talked with her. She agreed to leave for

Australia if she could have her jewels (which were in hock), if she could have some new clothes, have her passage paid and a couple hundred dollars in cash. I agreed to spend $1,000 on all this if she *really* wanted to go home. I didn't make the mistake of giving her all this money. I had everything arranged so that she had to be *on the boat* and at sea a full day before her jewels and the cash would be turned over to her by the purser. And I even gave money to the purser to send me a cable when all of this transaction had been completed.

"This was our agreement, Mae's and mine, and I was determined that it would be lived up to. As I expected, she tried to change it. She wanted the jewels and cash *before* she sailed, but I was adamant. Stan kept getting more and more nervous, and I could tell that all this was very wearing on him: would Mae go or wouldn't she? Would Stan go into a fit of depression or remorse? In order to prevent the latter, my brother, Murray, and I had set up a plan.

"Murray was to stay with Stan every minute of the day to divert him, to occupy his time during the week before Mae left. Now, there was this friend of my wife's, a good-looking blonde ingenue, Lois Neilson, who had worked at Vitagraph with Earl Montgomery and me in dozens of comedies—a very attractive girl and very *unlike* Mae. Lois and my wife, Louise, were in on my plan to prevent Stan from getting upset or depressed over Mae's departure.

"Finally the day for Mae's departure arrived. No one really knew if she would go or not. I remember it was a cold, miserable, rainy day in Los Angeles. My brother, Murray, had arranged to bring Stan over to meet Lois at her house. I was already there standing by a glowing log fire when Murray and Stan were invited in most graciously by Lois. Stan came right over to me and wanted to know at once if I had received the cable from the purser of Mae's ship saying that all was well. I said my wife had stayed at our house and would phone me as soon as the wire came. Stan could smell a roast cooking and he was most impressed with the homey look of Lois's bungalow. He was very surprised to learn that Lois had actually played in some of Stan's early comedies. Lois fixed a hot toddy for all of us and we sat around the fireplace.

"Stan and Murray soon dried out, and the smell of the cooking together with several hot drinks relaxed and soothed Stan. The phone rang. It was my wife and she read me the wire from the purser and I relayed it to Stan. Mae was now well on her way to Australia. Stan let out a yell and practically did a ballet leap. He grabbed me and Murray, hugged us, and actually had tears in his eyes—saying we were the two best friends he had ever had, even closer than his dad or brothers. He vowed to make for me the best comedies ever made."

One of the brightest comedies Stan made for Joe Rock was *Half a Man*, a two-reeler released in August 1925. It marks in most ways a progression in comic sensibilities over all previous Laurel efforts. Not that *Half a Man* is much touched by subtlety. Its pace is lethargic at times and gags are their own reason for being. But this is a film which shows Stan Laurel groping for comedy form, for a defined

47

character. Just as Chaplin had found the Tramp and made him gloriously his, so Stan was working for a comic identity. *Half a Man* suggests that if Oliver Hardy had not come along, Stan would probably have become something of a lively hybrid between Charlie Chaplin and Harry Langdon.

Certainly the Langdon strain is strong in this film which offers us a Stan drenched in innocence. As Winchell McSweeney, lollipop-loving scion of respectable fishing folk resident in New Tuna, Stan, sporting a giant fisherman's hat and saucer-sized pince-nez, receives from his folks the sad news that their depleted finances will force him to go out and seek his worldly fortunes. As Stan's mother tells him the sad news, tears trickle down her cheeks and Stan looks at them with interest, then holding out his hand, looks skyward to discover the source of the moisture. The bad news finally penetrates, and as Stan sobs at his mother's knee, he laps lustily at his lollipop.

Touching his fist nobly to his brow, putting his other hand bravely on his heart, he turns to leave and, head down, walks energetically into a suspended fishing net. He threshes madly about the beach for a time before he walks resolutely away, still enmeshed. Then, for no better reason than our need to be taken somewhere interesting, Stan boards a small craft just leaving the dock. Earlier in the film, Stan's mommy had warned him about girls—all girls—and the ship he boards is furnished with a dozen of them, nautically attired, and naughtily, aggressively, disposed toward Stan. With Langdon-like demeanor, he flees them until the head Amazon subdues him and carries him to the dinner table where she ties a napkin around his neck and literally spoon-feeds him. Now and later through the film Stan actually apes the Langdon overgrown-baby persona. (*Half a Man* was filmed the year Langdon had his first great Hollywood success. Stan frequently resorts to finger in mouth bewilderment and infantile stare, much like Langdon, albeit at more frenetic pace.)

As Stan eats his pablum, the motion of the ship induces seasickness, and along with everyone else, he goes to the railing for relief. This is a protracted gag which becomes rather nauseating in itself.

Stan next prepares to take a photograph of the crew. So vital was gag footage in these early comedy films that such subtleties as impelling motivations for action are cheerfully eschewed. At this point in the film we have no idea where the ship is headed, why the crew is primarily female, nor why Stan's presence on board is even tolerated. The reason for his taking the photograph is clear enough. It gives him the opportunity to set the ship on fire accidentally thereby giving the audience a diverting complication. He dives down into the bowels of the ship, coming back attired in every life jacket available on board. The girls escape in a lifeboat, the male sailors jump overboard—all literally clearing the decks to provide open stage for a prime Laurel gag. In a virtuoso display of mime, Stan approaches the side of the ship, knowing that he must jump, shakingly terrified at the prospect. His thrusts between go-and-stay, forward-and-recoil, are superbly executed—particularly in the use of his clenched hands which convulsively alternate between aiming a dive toward the water and supplicating a prayer heavenward.

Cut to a desert island where the girls have found sanctuary. Via title we are told there are only two times when women need men—day and night. Just as the girls seem doomed to their own company, Stan staggers up the beach and the girls cry, "*A man!*" It is here the film's title becomes operative because the cherubic, soggy Stan totters along, looking every other inch a man. The determined girls chase him down the beach, and in his virtuous quest for solitude, Stan reaches a cliff overlooking the sea. He threatens to hurl himself off if he is not left alone. They agree, pleading with him not to jump. He becomes their lord and master instantly.

Just as quickly, the girls spot the other male members of the crew finally reaching the island, something Stan does not see. At one point he petulantly threatens to jump again, and the head Amazon picks him up and throws him over the precipice herself. But because there are only a few seconds left in the last reel for a happy ending, Stan meets at cliff's bottom a fetching girl from the ship and they skip off down the beach together toward the "The End" title.

Half a Man was shot on location at Catalina Island, and in 1925 Catalina was just about the nicest place in California to be. Its unspoiled waters beating on a virtually virgin beach inspired Stan to craft the best moment in the picture. The child-like character he portrays cannot understand why the water flows forward toward the land, then recedes. This half a man does not grasp the reason for or even the fact of the ocean's rise and fall. At one point Stan skips down toward the water but is astounded when it chases him back up the beach. He turns sternly, extends his hands palms-front to the water in a cease-and-desist gesture—and the waters retreat. Secure in his victory, he shakes a reproving finger at the naughty water but he runs back again in astonished horror when the water disobeys and rushes him again. Stan runs back poutingly a few feet and when he turns, thinking he has gone far enough only to discover his feet still in water, he bends over and spanks the water in high indignation.

In the hands of anyone but a master pantomimist, all this would be fatuously childish, but Stan makes it convincing and, incredibly, quite charming. The character he creates is a febrile Langdon figure, almost an interesting person but unfortunately too derivative from the other comedian. What Stan needed at this point in his career was a comic form and a specific identity of his own. He was not yet ready to accommodate a partner, indeed he specifically refused one. Like most comic actors aiming for stardom, he needed to concentrate on establishing his own personality and this could easily be imperiled if his supporting actors were, so to speak, in his league. Not only Larry Semon but other comedians of the period justifiably regarded Stan as a scene-stealer and preferred not to work with him. Stan had now reached the point where *he* was wary of scene-stealers.

Joe Rock:

"Interestingly, although I had no intention of making them a team, I had wanted to use Babe Hardy in a number of the Stan Laurel comedies I made, but Stan always said no. Understandably, no top comic wanted to team with another comic unless that comic was willing to be either stooge, foil, or straight man—and whenever that kind of teaming was forced on comics—I mean equal teaming—it inevitably broke such teams up because of ego or jealousy problems. When I offered to bring Hardy into his pictures, Stan refused because he said that any heavy who played for laughs reduced the image of a heavy—and then really became a comic in competition with the star. I could understand Stan's refusal, of course, because at that time it did suggest the problem of direct competition. But the fact is if Hardy had been okayed by Stan at that point, the team of Laurel and Hardy might well have been created some time before they got together on the Roach lot. But I must emphasize that Stan didn't turn down my suggestion that Babe be brought in out of any dislike of Babe. Stan, after all, had known Babe from the old Vitagraph days especially when they were both playing parts in Larry Semon's comedies.

"In fact, that's when Stan first saw very real evidence of Babe Hardy's scene-stealing abilities. Stan could see that Babe was really putting it over on Semon who was not only acting but directing his own pictures as well. Semon just couldn't see when Babe would make some move with his head or other part of his body or with his derby or his tie to get a little extra attention from the audience. But the audience would notice it, of course, and they'd laugh like crazy, and this would infuriate Semon. In cutting the picture, he couldn't cut out Babe because Babe was actually in the scene with Semon. I couldn't convince Stan that it shouldn't make any difference if a heavy got some laughter, that in fact it would improve things. Stan still wasn't secure enough on his own to be able to share laughs. Later, of course, when he was teamed with Babe, he not only shared laughs with him but actually *built up* Babe's comedy in every way he could—and that's why they became the greatest comedy team in film history."

On the day Mae Laurel sailed for Australia, Stan lost a millstone around his neck and met his first wife. Joe Rock and his brother in arranging for Stan to receive the news of Mae's departure at Lois Neilson's did so with more than half an eye toward stimulating romance. The Rocks that day pretended to have engagements elsewhere and Lois generously asked Stan to stay for the meal she had been preparing. He did, and not long after, on August 23, 1926, Lois and Stan were married in Los Angeles. It was in that same year, 1926, when Stan went to the Hal Roach Studios for a protracted stay and screen immortality.

The boy with the Smile Wins

HAL ROACH Presents

Stan Laurel

in Two Part Comedies

You don't have to be told when a comedian is *good*; his comedies show it!

"Week End Party", Stan Laurel. "Good. Lots of laughs."—Guy C. Sawyer, Chester, Vt. (Herald)

"Roughest Africa", "If all the Laurel comedies are as good as this one, he's going to be a bet. Don't hesitate on these comedies. They're good."—Fred Holzapfel, Broadway Theatre, Minneapolis.

"Roughest Africa", "Immutably funny. A humdinger, sparkling with funny burlesque." —M. P. News.

"Roughest Africa" "Certain to bring peals of laughter from any audience."—Film Daily

"Frozen Hearts" "First class burlesque. Laurel is building a reputation for himself." —Trade Review.

Keep your eye on
Stan Laurel

Pathécomedy

A trade advertisement for an up-and-coming funster, 1923.

Two

Under the conditions of his 1925 contract with Joe Rock, Stan was to remain with Rock four years with annual salary increments. The Stan Laurel Comedies were very successful around the country and this did not escape the attention of Hal Roach.

Joe Rock:

"I knew Roach was talking to Stan. The world of film comedy was a pretty small one, and I kept hearing rumors that Stan was being approached not only by Roach but by a lot of the major studios as well. They all knew that with Mae gone and Stan happy, things were looking up for him. I also knew that I couldn't compete with the bigger studios when it came to salary. Stan could make a lot more money with them but, after all, he did have his contract with me, and in a very real sense, I made him.

"But when he got the better offer from Roach, I gave him his release simply because he wanted it. I could have taken it to court but what really would have been gained? We were —after all—friends, and we had done some awfully good work together."

And with that gentlemanly statement, Joe Rock authenticates not only his forthright character but his love of film comedy as well.* Rock knew that by the mid-1920s, the Hal Roach studio was a unique fount of comic creativity. By 1926, Roach had begun to assemble comedy artisans whose work, they little knew then, is likely to last as long as the motion picture itself. Artists like Charley Chase, Billy Gilbert, F. Richard Jones, the Our Gang kids, Leo McCarey, Edgar Kennedy, James Finlayson, Snub Pollard, and Oliver Hardy were crafting two-reel comedies of exceptional vitality and wit. So very versatile were the Roach actors that the boss did not work to create leading players, offering instead a group he billed as the Comedy All Stars. They were not all that by any means, but as a permanent stock comedy of highly talented comedians, they had few peers.

Stan, in joining this unit, met a group of men who rejoiced—there is no better word—in the creation of comedy. "It was like a perpetual party," Stan said. "Not that we didn't work hard, mind you. We didn't mind working overtime. In fact we never even *thought* of it as overtime when we wanted to perfect and shoot a gag which might take us well into the evening hours. I can't think of a better life than just making comedy or, when we weren't doing that, just sitting around and thinking and planning comedy."

One of those who thought about it, who crafted gags and occasionally directed Roach films of the 1920s was Frank

---

* Research has revealed that Rock did in fact file suit, and Laurel counter-sued, charging that Rock was preventing him from obtaining employment. The matter was resolved when Rock advised Roach late in 1926 that he had "no further claim on Mr. Laurel's services and he is completely released from any contract for the same."

Butler, later to win Hollywood renown as a Paramount script writer and author of the best Bing Crosby-Bob Hope "Road" pictures. Butler in a conversation with me recalled those days as ". . . sheer delight." *

Frank Butler:

"Utter fun, those days. To work at Roach's in the 1920s was something like an extended party. Everyone of the performers was not only allowed to contribute gag ideas, they were *expected* to. When Stan came to Roach's, he was hired principally as a performer, of course, but we quickly became aware that here was a first-rate comedy idea man. So he was invited to join our gag sessions.

"Were there any occasions more joyous in my life than those gag sessions? I suspect not. They were a joy. To paraphrase Falstaff, they were not only the cause of laughter in other people but laughable in themselves. Our chief gag man at Roach's in those early days was a man named Carl Harbaugh. Carl was very fond of the bottle which, however, he never, but never, allowed really to interfere with his work. But oh my, oh how many gag sessions he would come to with a princely hangover, unshaven, and consoling himself with endless dosings of Bromo. As I say, he never shaved, was voluminously profane and indescribably witty. On top of which he was an awfully nice guy.

"Carl lived and breathed gags. We usually had a daily session to construct the gags for films in work, and Carl presided over these sessions, throwing down Bromo or bicarb

* Frank Butler died June 10, 1967.

of soda, belching aggressively as he marshaled all our think-ing into something like a coherent story line.

"I can remember one gag session not long after I joined Roach, and it was a typical one. The session began with Carl picking up the thread of the story we had begun the previous time. He said: 'O.K.—now we've got this dame in her bedroom, and somehow we get this guy in the bedroom who wants to lay her. So, he starts to chase her, right? You figure out how we get this bastard into the house in the first place, Jerry, and we'll talk about that in a few minutes. O.K. The dame's in the bedroom, the hot pants guy is in the bed-room chasing her, so now we gotta complicate. O.K. Suppose —let's see—suppose the dame looks out the window and sees her husband coming up the walk into the house. O.K. She screams and faints, and of course the son of a bitch of a husband runs in the room and he sees the bastard who's been chasing his wife. The goddamn husband reaches under the sonofabitching table, pulls out an elephant tusk from under it and starts to beat the goddamn bejesus out of the hot pants guy. How's that for a beginning?'

"Please remember that I am a neophyte at all this. I felt a bit diffident about speaking up, but I did—for reasons of clarifying action and motivation, I *thought*. 'Excuse me, Mr. Harbaugh,' I said, 'but you say that the husband comes in, reaches under the table, pulls out an elephant tusk from there and then proceeds to beat up the would-be lover?' 'Right,' belched Carl. 'Well, pardon me,' I said, 'but just how did the elephant tusk come to be under the table in the first place?' 'How did it get there?' Carl asked wearily. 'It

got there because the goddamned property man *put it there!'*
and with that he went back to more vital matters.

"And so, early on, very early on, I learned that comedy on
the Roach lot—as on similar comedy lots in Hollywood—was
its own justification."

Frank Butler also remembered the genesis of the team of
Laurel and Hardy:

"Stan did very well as a performer, of course, and the fact
that he was invaluable in the gag sessions made him someone
rather special. In time it was realized that he would be a
natural as a director. As a result, he gradually phased himself
out of performing—which proved to be rather a surprise for
him. If someone had first told him on his arrival at Roach's
that a year or two later he wouldn't even want to perform,
I'm sure he'd have thought the guy was crazy. But Stan had
the deepest creative feelings of any of our actors on the lot,
and working as a gag man and director satisfied those feelings
very completely and proved exhilarating to boot.

"So it happened that when Stan was directing a Comedy
All Stars picture, *Get 'Em Young* in 1926, Babe Hardy was
playing the role of a butler. Stan had shot a little bit of the
film, and this was interrupted by a weekend. During which
Babe seriously hurt himself (he was a great amateur chef)
by spilling some scalding gravy from a leg of lamb over himself. Dick Jones—that was F. Richard Jones, production head
of the studio—tried frantically to get another comic to fill in
for Babe, but there was no one available on such short notice.
So Dick asked Stan to play the part. Stan was indebted to
Dick Jones because Dick had taught Stan many things

about film-making—the best way to set up shots, how to get the best camera angles, things like that—but Stan just didn't want to go back to performing. He was having too much fun as a writer-director. Dick then boosted Stan's salary considerably, and so Stan gave in and appeared in *Get 'Em Young.*

"That film was important for one thing other than marking Stan's return to performing: it was the film for which he invented one of his comedy staples—the whimpering cry. It got quite a laugh from the crew on the lot, so Stan made much of it, thereafter using it frequently and to good effect. Oddly, he never cared for it as humor, but he knew when to leave well enough alone, so it became part of his repertoire of comic tricks.

"Anyway, after doing *Get 'Em Young,* Stan thought he would return to his directing duties, but Dick Jones noted in *Get 'Em Young* an added dimension in Stan's playing not obvious before, an extra sense of wackiness (I guess you'd call it) which Stan had grown into. Dick asked Stan to become a comedian again. Stan resisted until Roach came through with an even larger raise, and Stan returned to performing in our very next picture."

That picture was *Slipping Wives,* the story of an artist, his beautiful wife, and a cardboard lover in the person of a paint salesman who is used by the wife to arouse her husband's dormant passions. There was also a comic butler in the cast. The cardboard lover and the butler were the supporting players. The film was rather ordinary but the two supporting players were not. One was Stan Laurel, the other was Oliver Hardy, and for the first time they were appearing together in a picture by Hal Roach.

Frank Butler:

"As to the identity of the person directly responsible for the teaming of Laurel and Hardy, let me be specific. It was Leo McCarey, and no one else, who created the team of Laurel and Hardy. As the Comedy All Star films were being made, Leo was the first among us to notice that putting the skinny fellow in juxtaposition with the fat fellow was not only nice contrast but very funny contrast. Roach, personally, didn't create Laurel and Hardy as a team. At the time Leo first thought of giving the boys the biggest roles in the All Star series, Roach was on an around-the-world tour. Of course when Hal came back, he thoroughly approved. The first film in which Laurel and Hardy really attained a basic kind of dimension was an item called *Duck Soup*. Then they made others, of course, within the Comedy All Stars format until their first official Laurel and Hardy team film, *Putting Pants on Philip,* which was made in 1927. Leo really put the boys on the same path together, and set many of the basic plots for their early films.

"As to the type of characters Stan and Babe became in their films, the underlying concept—their invincible dumbness—came from Stan. He was the first one to bring that idea into play at the gag sessions, and Leo and the gag men took up that concept and spun out infinite variations on it."

In an interview with Leo McCarey, I asked him how the modus operandi of crafting the early Laurel and Hardy pictures came about. With high good humor, he recalled those days as among the pleasantest in his life.

Leo McCarey:

"Stan had one of the best and most inventive comedy minds in history—I'm most happy to say that. I worked with him smoothly and sympathetically, and that made it very easy for us to meet the studio's rather demanding deadlines. We were usually expected to turn out a *good* two-reeler in two weeks, although sometimes of course we either went over or under that.

"There was one interesting thing about Stan's salary, by the way. He always insisted on getting twice as much money as Babe—*not* I must emphasize because he thought he was twice as funny as Babe—but because he was doing twice as much work as Babe, and Babe agreed with him. When the end of the shooting day came for Babe, he'd be out on the golf course, but Stan would be starting almost another full day of work—working on gags and story with me or helping cut the picture.

"After I got the boys going as a team, something funny happened to me. I had to take over supervision of all Roach pictures after Dick Jones left and this meant a wide variety of films and comedians and directors to be directly concerned with—yet I found myself spending almost every waking hour thinking of Laurel and Hardy, those two wonderful *characters*, not the boys who played them, Stan and Babe. Almost everything that happened to me during the day, I'd some way or another tie up with Laurel and Hardy, consciously or unconsciously. Getting into my car I'd think of the boys and what trouble they'd get into with a car. Passing a bus I'd think of them causing a rumpus on that bus. Seeing an advertisement in a newspaper for a cabaret, I'd think of them going there and wreaking havoc. One time I had to get a tooth extracted, and while I was lying down waiting for the Novocain to take effect, my eye caught a reproduction of Gainsborough's painting of the Blue Boy on the dentist's wall, and I thought to myself, 'Now, how can I possibly work the Blue Boy into a Laurel and Hardy picture?'

"After a few minutes' thought, it was easy. To relieve myself of pain while the doctor was tugging away, I began to plot a plot with Stan, Ollie, and Blue Boy. I had the boys working in a stable, and they happen to hear the news that Blue Boy has been stolen, and that a big reward is available. Now, this is the painting that's been stolen, of course, but the boys don't know this. As it happens, there is a *horse* named Blue Boy in the boys' stable, and they naturally think it's the return of the horse that will net the big reward. So they go to the gorgeous mansion of the millionaire who has had the painting stolen. This fellow is upstairs, the boys shout out they've got Blue Boy and the millionaire yells out happily, 'Put it on the piano!'—and the boys double take, of course, and they have a merry time trying to get that horse up on the grand piano. And all of this came from my toothache!

"But that's how a lot of the gags and stories came from— just from some little thought we'd bring to the gag sessions, a thought we'd sit down and chew over and expand upon.

Once I came back from a trip to New York where I'd been to a dinner party at which—for fun—a number of us had gone around pulling each other's bow ties, snapping them out of their knots. Just a silly thing to do, a little bit of fun. But when I came back to Los Angeles, I remembered that as being a perfect gag for the boys, so that's how the Laurel and Hardy tit-for-tat began."*

The tit-for-tat gag, the one in which mutually administered physical indignity between two or more people is consummated at deliberate and unhurried pace became a Laurel and Hardy staple through the years.

This gag—the protracted and more frenzied extensions of which I term "reciprocal destruction"—became a Laurel and Hardy gag hallmark. For Stan, gags were the essential texture of Laurel and Hardy and everything in their films of deep value, in his view, depended on them. As the chief architect of those gags in their formative days as a team, he realized the necessity for a simple story as essential background, but his greatest creative pleasure lay in gag construction.

By the mid-1930s, the Laurel and Hardy characters had attained their permanent form. They were, first of all, two supremely brainless men, totally innocent of heart and almost outrageously optimistic. Their bowler hats crowned their essential dignity, and the use and misuse of these hats were the activations of their unceasing battle to maintain that

* McCarey carried his humor with him when he left Roach in 1929. The tit-for-tat gag can be seen in his 1930 Paramount film, *Let's Go Native*. For additional comment on Leo McCarey, see appendix.

With George Rowe in "Near Dublin," a 1923 Hal Roach comedy.

Stan in "The Sleuth," a 1925 Joe Rock comedy.

An embryonic Laurel and Hardy in "Slipping Wives," filmed in 1926.

Clowning on the Hal Roach lot, between filmmaking chores.

"The boys" with director James Parrott, circa 1928.

With wife Lois, and the baby daughter named after her.

With Josephine the monkey on the set of "Two Tars," 1928.

dignity. Certain gestures, movements, and spoken phrases became indelible trade marks: Stanley's armfold fall, his flat-footed walk (an effect created by wearing army shoes with heels removed), his baby cry, his vacuous eye blink, his elaborate head scratch which pulled up his hair to form a natural fright wig; Ollie's vast delicacy of gesture as seen in extended pinky and gracious hat tip, his embarrassed tie twiddle, his grandiose, rococo signature on documents, his look of exasperated frustration made directly to the camera following a Laurel misadventure, his imperious finger point to Stan either to remove his hat or his person elsewhere. Ollie was always to go first even if, as happened always, this arrangement led to disaster. Ollie was "smarter" than Stanley yet he was infinitely dumber because, despite this invincible ignorance, he always *thought* he was smarter. In Babe's own opinion of his character, "There is no one as dumb as a dumb guy who thinks he's smart." These two characters are the definition of friendship, living in a life framework of hopes perpetually deferred yet hourly renewed—the ultimate optimists. "Why don't you do something to *help* me?" Ollie asks Stan, who does—pushing them both therewith into new catastrophe. The Hardy lament which most characteristically identified the team's essence is "Here's *another* fine mess[*] you've gotten me into!" Those messes delighted millions, particularly during the Depression years when the troubles of the day were diminished by empathizing with the troubles of these two lovable dimwits and their everyday frustrations writ large.

As the 1930s began, the Hal Roach studios created a

[*] Hardy's oft-repeated sentiment was actually, "Here's another *nice* mess..." despite the title of their 1930 film, *Another Fine Mess*.

number of profitable comedy series: the Patsy Kelly-Thelma Todd films, the Our Gang films, the Charley Chase films (the wonderful and currently much undervalued and neglected Charley Chase!), and the Laurel and Hardy films. Of these, the latter were the most profitable for Roach. Yet Laurel and Hardy received hardly any attention from the critics principally because the team made only two- and three-reel comedies which inevitably placed them in the "added attraction" category. Notwithstanding, the hold on the affections of most American filmgoers was strong and constantly growing.

Laurel and Hardy had become famous but were not aware of it. In 1932 they decided to take a vacation together in England. After an uneventful train trip they reached Chicago where they were to change trains for New York. Without warning they were caught in a surging mass of fans, photographers, and reporters.

Stan:

"It was unbelievable. Babe and I just didn't have an idea, I guess, how many people had been seeing our pictures over the years. We were actually frightened by seeing so many people—and it kept up wherever we went: in New York there were newsreel cars following us down Broadway; the docks at Southampton were filled with mobs of people, all whistling our theme song ['The Dance of the Cuckoos']; and London had even bigger crowds. All over England, Scotland—even France where we thought we might get a bit of relief from it—crowds everywhere. Not that we were really anything but very pleased by the whole thing, but we were just so stunned by it all. We didn't even get our vacation as it turned out. We came back to California and to work just to get a rest."

What Stan also came back to was marital discord. His marriage to Lois Neilson had seemed exemplary. As a former film comedy actress, she had ample reason to know his professional life and the time demands made by it. There is no evidence that she was anything other than an agreeable and understanding helpmeet. A daughter, Lois Jr., was born to the Laurels in 1928.* In May 1930 a son, Stan Jr., was born, but lived only a few weeks. The first intimations of trouble in the Laurel marriage came in May 1933 when Mrs. Laurel filed suit for divorce, stating in the complaint that her husband advised her to get a divorce, said he did not love her and ignored her at parties. The Laurels were reconciled in August of that year, Stan crediting the reunion to the existence of his daughter. However, on September 10, 1935, a divorce was executed. The only comment Stan ever made either in public or private on his first marriage appeared in *Movie Classic* magazine.

Stan:

"When two people reach the place in life where they can no longer share a laugh together, then it is practically impossible to share the same bed and board. Laughter is not a trivial part of married life. To the contrary, it is very important. Neither my wife nor I considered the idea of divorce lightly. We have a little five-year-old daughter and for her

---

* Daughter Lois' correct date of birth is December 10, 1927.

sake, as well as our own, we both sincerely attempted to make a go of our marriage . . . We reached the point where we were continually getting on each other's nerves. I'm sure that nothing I did was very amusing to my wife. When we were first married, little annoying things that we both might do were laughed off and forgotten. But in the past year we seem to have lost that saving grace of humor. When we realized that we had reached the point where we could no longer laugh together, then there was nothing else to do—difficult though it was for us both—but legally separate. That's really the whole story."

This is hardly a very revealing statement, but given the blandness of the times in respect to public announcements of separation and Stan's innate reticence, it is a wonder it was given at all. The prime point established—Stan's inability to share his sense of humor with Lois—is certainly one of the reasons for their split.

In later years, after Stan had been blessed with a warm and enduring marriage, I was to discover that he would talk about anything under the sun but his marital history. The subject gave him much pain. I can recall vividly one day when his mail came, he picked up the current edition of *Newsweek*. Then as now the magazine had a feature column, "Where Are They Now?" which brought readers up to date on the current whereabouts and life situations of famous people no longer in the news. The column that issue was devoted to Stan, dwelling at some length on his marital misadventures. As I watched him read the piece, his face fell and stamped plain on that expressive countenance was something I had never seen on it before—real pain. I didn't know what he was reading but it was manifestly distressing. He frowned, then wordlessly pushed the magazine over to me, one finger disdainfully tapping the page containing the article. I read it (the facts were already well known to me), and I set it down, not knowing what to say. But I should have known that this great gentleman's sense of humor was indestructible. "Now *that*," he said, pointing to the article, "that would make a hell of a good Charlie Chan movie!" Whereupon uproarious laughter from us both, and the matter was decently buried.

In exhuming it here, I do so principally for the record. So much has been written in gaudy Sunday supplements about the "much-married" Stan Laurel that it is necessary to put at least the basic facts in order. The dramatis personae in these proceedings are the following:

Lois Neilson

Virginia Ruth Rogers, a Los Angeles widow

Vera Ivanova Shuvalova, a Russian singer, dancer, dancer and putative countess, known professionally as Illeana

Ida Kitaeva Raphael, Russian opera singer and actress.

The sequence of Stan's marriages and divorces:

Lois

LEGAL MARRIAGE: 1926
DIVORCE: 1935

Virginia Ruth

> WEDDING CEREMONY: 1934
>
> LEGAL MARRIAGE: 1935 (First ceremony with Virginia Ruth invalid because decree from Lois not final.)
>
> DIVORCE: 1937
>
> LEGAL MARRIAGE: 1941
>
> DIVORCE: 1946

Illeana

> LEGAL MARRIAGE: 1938 (January 1)
>
> WEDDING CEREMONY: 1938 (February 28, based on the groundless fear his first ceremony to Illeana was not valid.)
>
> WEDDING CEREMONY: 1938 (April 26, in a Russian Orthodox church ceremony to please Illeana.)
>
> DIVORCE: 1940

Ida

> LEGAL MARRIAGE: 1946

For anyone able to count, this makes clear that Stan had four wives and was married a total of five times, although he went through eight wedding ceremonies. Newspaper headlines, therefore, like STAN LAUREL MARRIES EIGHTH TIME are interesting but inaccurate. One reason his marriages attracted so much press attention was because of bizarre incidents like Virginia Ruth's picketing Stan and Illeana's honeymoon suite on the grounds that their union was bigamous. It was not, but this statement was enough to send Stan apprehensively back to the judge for another ceremony. Additionally, Illeana was a colorful lady with a scarlet temper who on more than one occasion hit Stan over the head with a large frying pan. Illeana, operating on the theory that any publicity was good publicity, was not averse to giving details of their marital squabble to reporters.

In speaking of what at least on paper seems to be a checkered marital record, Frank Butler offered perhaps the most cogent evaluation of it to date.

Frank Butler:

"Stan was what one of his wives called a marrying type. 'A good boy but he has a marrying complex,' I believe is the way she described him to the reporters one day. Well, that was quite right, but it was an honorable complex, maybe *too* honorable a complex. I am of the opinion that one or two of these ladies Stan might much more profitably have retained as mistresses. But he was much too honorable a man for that. When he fell in love, it was all the way, and he insisted on marriage—and I am speaking very carefully when I say that in a very real sense, he was too honorable for his own good."

The one area of Stan's life where discord did not obtrude was the one before the camera, at least in the prime years with Roach. During the late 1920s, Laurel and Hardy concentrated on making two- and three-reelers of distinction. Some of these silent films are unarguably classics, unlikely to be surpassed in comedic content even by Charlie Chaplin. In *Big Business* (1929), Stan and Ollie are selling Christmas trees to a number of stoutly resistant Californians. One of these is the redoubtable James Finlayson—"Fin" the formidable—whose irritation at the boys' persistence in personality salesmanship grows into a mounting frenzy of reciprocal destruction as he vengefully, piece by piece, destroys Stan and Ollie's Model T Ford as they vengefully, piece by piece, destroy his house. If this were sheer demolition, it would be only mildly amusing; but so demonic is "Fin's" retributory vengeance on the boys' car—so scamperingly gleeful are Stan and Ollie as they tear "Fin's" house apart bit by solid bit that total comic euphoria prevails. It is hardly presumptuous to call *Big Business* one of the ten best short comedy films ever made. Similar to it in nuance and a trifle richer in characterization of supporting players is *Two Tars* (1928) in which the boys as sailors out on the town rent a tin lizzie, pick up two giddy flappers and take them out on a joy ride which ends in a stupendous orgy of reciprocal destruction. On a country road the two displaced seafarers are caught in a temporary roadblock with a score of other cars. In the process of extricating their Ford from this line-up, the boys reverse themselves accidentally into the car driven by testy Edgar Kennedy, who promptly seeks full-dimensional retribution, which must of course be answered in kind. A neighbor car is hit in the process, which in turn spreads the madness of reciprocal destruction from car to car. The catalysts of all this are Stan and Ollie, adventurers in catastrophe, who, stimulated by the admiring glances of their doxies, precipitate anarchy until, as limned vividly in a beautifully composed long shot near the end of the film, utter chaos is triumphant for a full half mile. *Two Tars* has peers among short film comedies; it is not likely to have a superior.

When sound came to Hollywood, Laurel and Hardy acknowledged it in a pleasant jest by entitling their first film in this genre, *Unaccustomed As We Are.* They did not share in the frenzied fear that seized many performers in the silent film. Because both men had received their early training in show business before live audiences (Hardy had toured in minstrel shows and did much cabaret work in Florida), speaking lines held no terror for them. They continued with two- and three-reel films until 1935, Stan particularly enjoying the creation of these shorter-length comedies. "There is just so much comedy we can do along a certain line and then it gets to be unfunny," was his comment when asked why he objected to playing in feature length pictures.

The best of the Laurel and Hardy sound shorts is a three-reeler, *The Music Box,* which brought Laurel and Hardy their only Academy Award as the best short subject of 1932. Typical of their short films, it has a single, simple concept for its story line: the boys move a boxed player piano up a high rise of terraced steps. The fascinating variety of changes in their frustrations as they haul, push, strain, lose control, go forward and backward precipitately, is totally captivating and impermeably hilarious, even after countless viewings. It is a film for the ages, an act of simple, well-crafted genius. As successful as *The Music Box* was, Hal Roach realized that feature films were much more profitable, and he steered Laurel and Hardy that way despite Stan's frequently stated preference for the shorter form.

But Stan realized that the short subject was yearly slipping in favor with the exhibitors as the double-feature program became increasingly a fact of life. From the mid-1930s on, Laurel and Hardy devoted themselves to feature films, and of these Stan much preferred the films in which the boys appeared in costume against a colorful background of the past, with attendant music and song. Typical of such efforts is *The Devil's Brother* (1933), an enchanting burlesque of Auber's opera *Fra Diavolo*, in which Laurel and Hardy appear as Stanlio and Ollio, two charmingly simple sods in eighteenth-century Italy who are dragooned into being bandits. Stan was especially exhilarated by costume pictures. Although there were several good Laurel and Hardy features done in contemporary ambience—notably *Sons of the Desert* (1934) and *Block-Heads* (1938)—Stan loved period pieces because as he told me ". . . there's so much more that one can do in the way of production values in those costume pictures—like the costumes themselves, of course, the pretty sets and the music. I've always enjoyed that—a mixture of color and humor—because it reminds me so much of the English pantomimes I've loved from the time I first saw one at age three." These pantomimes remained in Stan's memory all his life, and they were to serve as the models for the projected television films Laurel and Hardy were contracted for before illness and death terminated their partnership.

As counterpoint to Stan's marriage troubles, there were also certain discords in his professional life—with management, never with Hardy. To some extent Hardy was the unwitting cause of dissension between Stan and Hal Roach in

74

Relaxing with Hal Roach, during the filming of "Pardon Us" in 1930.

Sailing to England on the Aquitania, 1932; with Stan's stepmother, Venitia, and his father, A.J. Jefferson, in Southhampton.

Mugging for the camera on the S.S. Paris, en route to New York, 1932.

With director William Seiter between takes on "Sons of the Desert," 1933.

With actor David Leland on the set of "Nothing But Trouble," 1944.

that Hardy was always kept under separate contract from Stan. This was a normal enough situation in the beginning of the boys' careers. Roach had not hired them as a team and separate contracts were entirely sensible until the time came, as it did, when they were irrefrangibly a team. Keeping both men under separate contract was a shrewd business move by Roach. As Stan said, "I can't blame him for that, I suppose, but I certainly couldn't agree with him. Keeping us under separate contract meant that he could control us completely, bargain with each of us individually. Whereas if we were a team contractually, if we were a legal entity, he would find it much more difficult to maneuver a deal to his special advantage. Now, I don't mean Hal was ever dishonest with us, or tried to gyp us. We were always well paid. But we could have made more money and had greater freedom if we had been legally a team long before we were." This did not occur until 1940 when Laurel and Hardy Feature Productions was incorporated but by then it was too late for freedom. The company was never to make a film.

Throughout the 1930s, Stan fought a continuing round of actions with the Roach company. The scenario was unvarying: Babe Hardy's contract expired a year before Stan's and Roach would offer Hardy an increased sum to renew the contract; Hardy would sign; a year later Roach would offer Stan an increase on his new contract; Stan would refuse; Roach and Stan would huddle and a few days later, a satisfactory arrangement (much more money for Stan) would be announced. At times these disputes reached public notice,

as on March 15, 1935, when the Roach studios announced
that the team of Laurel and Hardy would be no more. Less
than three weeks later it was announced that Stan had
signed his new contract with Roach. In the years that followed, this pattern was repeated until Stan became determined that at least he would never again sign a Roach
contract unless it coincided with Hardy's. In 1939, at the ter-
minus of his contract, Stan decided to wait until Hardy could
sign with him, and for most of that year only Hardy was on
the Roach payroll. Roach decided to see if Hardy could be
teamed with someone else, and the someone else as it turned
out was a splendid comedian, Harry Langdon, then under
Roach contract. But *Zenobia,* the film which Hardy and
Langdon made, was an exercise in dullness, and in 1939
Roach signed Laurel and Hardy, now in tandem legally, to
do two new films. After these pictures, the urge to return to
his first love, vaudeville, seized Stan and he wrote a sketch
in which he and Hardy go to a police station for drivers'
licenses. They toured the sketch cross country, together with
a number of variety acts and a line of girls, in a full-length
show called *The Laurel and Hardy Revue.*

In 1941, partially because Stan and Hal Roach were too
tired of the protracted salary wrangles over recent years and
also because Stan thought he might find wider horizons at
another studio, Laurel and Hardy went over to 20th Century-Fox. The contemplated wider horizons diminished to
tunnel vision. Stan had argued with Roach over salary and
had endured occasional pointless editing of comedy footage
from Roach sources, but by and large Hal Roach had left

Stan to his own devices. Roach also had the curious idea that Stan was notably deficient in feature film story-line concepts, an idea not exactly substantiated by the existence in Laurel and Hardy films of many beguiling story lines.* But the very fact that Roach allowed Stan to more or less (and mostly more) make films the way he wanted is high tribute to the producer.

At 20th Century-Fox, a totally different atmosphere prevailed. Here Stan began work on his films as he always did with some exhaustive sessions on story and gags. To his deep consternation he found the studio heads at Fox not primarily interested in profits but *only* interested in profits. Stan and Roach, whatever their differences, were one in their love for comedy and Roach would "spare no expense" to create it. Hal Roach needs no finer monument than the vast footage of first rate comedy bearing his name. This was no accident. Money had to be spent to create money. But at Fox, Stan was told at once that he had no autonomy. He was to do pictures the studio way or not at all. If Stan had an idea for constructing a set which would enhance a particular gag, he was told brusquely that there was too much expense involved, that there was no reason why all the Laurel and

* In 1973 I asked George Marshall, who had directed several excellent Laurel and Hardy films, what he thought of Stan's ability in story construction. "Excellent," said Marshall. "And by the same token, Roach was rather deficient along this line. He would suggest the vaguest outline of a story, say 'Know what I mean?' and then walk away, leaving us to try and figure out what in hell he *did* mean. So we just went ahead and did our own stories. Stan was always very instrumental in getting these stories together. Actually he was never too much interested in story as such; he was more concerned with dreaming up those wonderful gags."

Hardy gags could not be played within conventional sets. "Look, you can do them in any goddamn room," one executive told Stan. Thus the buck besting the brain.

A case in point was the preparation for the film, *The Big Noise* (1944). For a necessary travel sequence, Stan accepted, with qualification, the idea from one of the Fox gag men that the scene in the Roach film *Berth Marks* (1929) in which Stan and Ollie share a claustrophobic upper berth be repeated. "O.K.," Stan told the Fox writers, "I would much rather have a brand new gag, but if you want that one so much, we can re-use it, only let's make it better this time. The first time we used that gag, Babe and I were sweating and stretching out in that berth trying to find room where there wasn't any, and getting all tangled up with ourselves. We can make that even funnier today by putting the berth in a transcontinental airliner. That'll add an entirely new angle to the gag. We'll have the airplane hit some air pockets and the up-and-down movements of the berth can make some of those arm and leg entanglements of ours very funny." Stan was told coldly that discussion on the matter was pointless, that the scene would work perfectly well in the old setting. Stan attempted to point out that the new gag was much funnier and that building the airplane berth would not be expensive. He was rudely ignored.

If this were an exceptional instance of the studio's over-all attitude a man mild-mannered as Stan could have borne it with some equanimity, but such obtuse behavior was absolutely typical of 20th Century-Fox during the making of the six Laurel and Hardy films on that lot in 1941–45. During those years the boys also made two films for Metro-Gold-wyn-Mayer where much the same do-it-our-way-only attitude prevailed. These eight films, excepting possibly the Fox 1943 film, *Jitterbugs*, are artistic disgraces. They contain any number of old Laurel and Hardy routines from the Roach days but these have an air of strain about them and were used only on studio insistence. As in the instance of the upper berth gag, the Fox people wanted Stan to churn out footage at a rapid rate and (they explained to him) the easiest way to do that was by repeating old formulas literally. Stan did not object to the use of old gags because he knew certain of their routines were hallmarks of their style, much beloved of the fans. What Stan objected to vehemently was the studio's refusal to flavor these gags with newer sauces.

"Inevitably, too," says William K. Everson speaking of those films, "Laurel and Hardy were growing old—and age can be a terrible thing for a comedian like Stan Laurel, whose forte is the projection of innocence. The added years hardly affected Oliver Hardy, whose screen image could logically mellow and mature with him . . . But there were certain clowns to whom youth was essential—Stan Laurel, Harry Langdon, Buster Keaton. Once lines began to crease those baby-like features and weight was added to their bodies, they were no longer the believable innocents, but instead old men retreating into infantilism." This is true enough, but by 1944 it was not Stan's age so much as the tensions of working in films he despised and his marital troubles which began to show in his face. Almost miraculously those signs of tension and the mark of subsequent illness were to be erased from his face for the last decade of his life. Before that placid time, however, there was still one more film for Laurel and Hardy to do—another dreadful film—their last, shot in France. *Atoll K.*

Ida Laurel has pungent memories of that unhappy experience. *

Ida Laurel:

"I'm hardly likely to forget the date we left for France and the date we returned—April 1, 1950, and April 1, 1951. But there was no April Fooling about that terrible year. That bloody picture was supposed to take twelve weeks to make, and it took twelve months. We got to Paris, feeling wonderful, all set to go, and the producer told Stan there was not even the beginning of a story ready. Also in Paris we met Leo Joannon, the director. In France, the director is everything, and we soon realized this. But even Joannon had no idea of a story for a film. Moreover, Joannon was to be in complete charge. Stan was not happy about that. Stan then got together with the writers, but *they* had no ideas for a story. Imagine! Of course that worried Stan very much. So we just sat around and waited. Then Stan decided to write the story with two writers from the States, one of whom, I recall, was Monte Collins. They came. The French writers always slept until ten each day, and they'd even *miss* days. Stan wasn't used to this. It was all very casual. They started to shoot the picture first in Paris, then on location which was on an island between Cannes and St. Raphaël.

"The director, Joannon, dressed himself up like Cecil B.

* Ida Laurel died January 26, 1980.

De Mille—puttees, pith helmet and carried a megaphone—everything. Honest to God. Stan used to say, 'Joannon is funnier than the picture—although *that's* not saying a hell of a lot.' Stan couldn't get over those megaphones Joannon carried. He carried a different one for each occasion. Another thing: Joannon liked to take films of the water. Just of the water, that's all. Stan used to say, 'I guess he just *likes* water. Maybe because this is the story of an island Joannon thinks it's important to take a lot of water shots. Only he ought to get the island in there, too.' Stan remembered this Joannon spending *three* days shooting a lake because it was the most photogenic lake he'd ever seen. My God! Anyway, Joannon seemed to know nothing about making a movie—nothing.

"And the whole production set-up was beyond belief. If Stan wanted just a little prop, they'd have to send to Paris for it. I mean little, little things. Like a pencil sharpener, for instance—they'd have to send to *Paris*. My God, it was awful.

"Then Stan started to get ill. The doctor was worse than the director. Didn't know what he was doing. Stan was in terrible pain, he couldn't urinate, he was really ill. Ben Shipman, Stan's lawyer and old friend, came over, saw that the director was awful, so Ben got one of Stan's old friends, Alf Goulding (who'd directed the boys in *A Chump at Oxford*) to come over from England so that Stan could at least tell the director what to do as a director should. And on top of everything there was this terrible, exhausting heat. During all of this the bloody director kept shooting lakes, hills, lakes, *everything* except poor Stan and Babe—who were waiting around in their make-up. It was unbelievable.

"Finally Stan got so ill he had to go to the hospital, and there a whole bunch of doctors examined him. They couldn't find out what was wrong—all those doctors, imagine. Stan got very, very bad. Then a famous medical professor came in and operated at once. The other doctors had been afraid to operate because it had been discovered that Stan had diabetes. But this new doctor did an exploratory operation and it was found that Stan had something like a boil on his prostate.

"But even with all that pain—and there had been so much of it and for such a long time—he was so funny. Just before the nurses took him to the operating room, they gave him a shot to put him to sleep. Then we waited a while for it to take effect, and then two nurses and I started to take Stan up on the elevator to the operating room. He was very quiet, and then he said loud and very brightly, 'But I'm not sleepy —I can hear you!'—in such a funny way.

"He had the operation—then three nurses around the clock. I stayed at the hospital around the clock, too—*comme une chienne* the French newspapers described me. Gradually, his wound healed, but he couldn't speak French so I had to translate for him all the time, night and day. I even had to change his bandages sometimes. Gradually, he got better, but not really an awful lot better. He went back to the picture on location at that bloody island and this time he got dysentery because the food we were served there was so bad. He went down from 165 pounds to 114. They put up a little hospital on the set, and he would work in little spurts —twenty minutes here, a half hour there. You can see in the film how bad he looks. On April 1, 1951, we left France, and he was still ill. Gradually our own doctor in California helped him get well and gain weight but it took months. That was *Atoll K* for you!"

Atoll K is an execrable film. No Laurel and Hardy film exists without some cause for laughter in it, and some fun can be found in this tired pseudo-satire about an island utopia which the boys found. But it is a sad comedown for the funniest team in film comedy, a dishearteningly dull swan song.

It would be unendurable to think that *Atoll K* was the final contribution of Laurel and Hardy to the world of entertainment. Fortunately for their psychological well-being after the 20th Century-Fox experience, they had been invited by an English impresario, Bernard Delfont, to make a 1947 vaudeville tour of the British Isles. This was a tremendously successful tour which featured their drivers' license sketch, and after the debacle of *Atoll K*, they were warmly receptive to Delfont's offer to repeat the engagement in 1952. For this tour, Stan wrote a new sketch based on a 1930 two-reeler of theirs, *Night Owls*, a sketch he later destroyed* because of its inadequacy, but which gave him much pleasure in playing at the time. They made yet another triumphal British tour with a newly written sketch of Stan's, *Birds of a Feather*, in 1953 which was the year I met Stan backstage at the Hippodrome Theatre, Birmingham. A graduate student at the nearby Shakespeare Institute at Stratford-upon-Avon, I frequently came to Birmingham for work in the library there, and on one of these occasions I found to my delight

---

* Fortunately, a copy of this sketch still exists. See Appendix C.

that Laurel and Hardy were appearing in person. A Laurel and Hardy buff from childhood, I went to see *Birds of a Feather*, was suitably entranced, and impulsively went backstage to meet them. Because I was a total stranger and statusless, I was prepared to receive a pleasant but cursory reception. The reception was more than pleasant and far from cursory; moreover, as I was to learn, it was the reception they gave everyone. When I realized that the charm and old-fashioned courtesy of both men were totally real, it sealed my lifelong affection for them forever. I suspect that people who love Laurel and Hardy sense that at the heart of those two unique screen personalities exist two warmhearted and deep-souled human beings. Such is the fact.

During the Birmingham engagement, I saw Stan every day, at his invitation, because we shared a common passion —the celebration of humor. I questioned him at great length. I was intensely curious about his professional life and his ideas on humor, so much so that after a few days I felt I was overdoing it rather. He not only failed to mind the extended questioning but clearly relished it. My writing hand grew weary but all that fortnight and at various other places in England and the United States, I pursued my note-taking until I had adequate material to write *Mr. Laurel and Mr. Hardy*. Publication of the book by Doubleday in 1961 and above all the frequent showings of Laurel and Hardy films on television during the 1960s began to increase his fan mail to an unprecedented degree. "How I wish I could answer them all with a big, long letter," he said, "but there's just no way to do that. I deeply appreciate it but it's physically impossible. The people who write are so damned nice, you feel obligated. Many of them want to become pen pals, and I write saying I'd like to hear from them occasionally. However, I do write consistently to collectors of Laurel and Hardy films because I have an obligation to them."

That the names of Laurel and Hardy had become institutionalized, that the two of them seemed likely to enter the pantheon of great world entertainers, was always a marvel to Stan. "Odd, isn't it?" he once said to me. "We just wanted to bring a few laughs to people, and then—all that public attention and love! Unbelievable. I guess it just proves what I've always believed—that people need laughter like they need food."

On tour with "The Driver's License Sketch."

Three

Although the craft of sketch-writing has not (praise be) gone from the earth, it is in many ways a vanishing skill. To present a ludicrous human situation in ten to twenty memorable minutes calls for a special expertise which demands not only wit, but wit's soul, brevity. The number of skilled sketch writers is not legion. But those who know the craft well have rather easily made the career transition to top rank farce-comedy playwrights, as witness George M. Cohan, George S. Kaufman, and Neil Simon. These men share with Stan Laurel a joyously aggressive sense of the ludicrous.

Stan's father, A.J., was a prolific sketch creator, writing them not only for himself in his early music hall days but frequently on commission for other farceurs over the years. Stan inherited his father's knack in turning out these slight but vastly entertaining pieces, an affection for this form of creativity leading him to become a Hollywood gag man of pre-eminent order. While Hal Roach unjustifiably considered Stan a poor man on story, he praised him to the heights as a gag man. "There was no better creator of gags than Stan Laurel," Roach said. "None better—in the world."

In the four sketches following, Stan was, of course, writing for the characters of Laurel and Hardy as they had ultimately

become: two innocent, spectacularly bumbling, splendidly ig-
norant, unfailingly optimistic men. There is an implicit dan-
ger in reading—as opposed to seeing—these sketches for anyone who is not familiar with the sound and inflection of the
voices of Laurel and Hardy. A reader is also similarly disadvantaged if he cannot summon to memory the sight of Stan
and Ollie—the simple, trusting vacuity of one, the assertive
lordliness of the other. With a caution, then, that two of these
sketches were written to be spoken and seen rather than read,
two were written only to be heard, and that in any case these
words on paper are to the reality of Laurel and Hardy as the
musical score is to the living orchestra, herewith the only
four extant examples of Stan's sketch-writing talents. *

LAUREL AND HARDY VISIT LONDON (1932)

(This brief sketch was written for a Columbia Graphophone
Ltd. recording which Stan and Babe made during their first
visit to England as a team. Stan wrote it in a few minutes
while waiting for the recording equipment to be set up.)

OLLIE: Ladies and gentlemen, this is Oliver Hardy speaking.
I am taking this opportunity of thanking you and the
countless friends we have in the British Isles for the
wonderfully warmhearted reception you have given me
on my first visit to your beautiful country. Words cannot
describe my feelings—

STAN: Hey.

OLLIE: Never before have I been received—

* See the appendix for "On the Spot" (1952).

STAN: Hey!

OLLIE: Never before have I been—

STAN: (*Whistles to gain attention.*)

OLLIE: Pardon me, ladies and gentlemen, I think my friend, Mr. Laurel, wishes to speak to me. What's on your mind?

STAN: What about mentioning me in the speech?

OLLIE: Don't worry, I'll get to you in just a few minutes.

STAN: In a few minutes?

OLLIE: Certainly.

STAN: Well, the record will be over in a few minutes, then you won't be able—

OLLIE: Listen, why don't you do something to *help* me?

STAN: Well, what can I do?

OLLIE: Here, here's a hard-boiled egg. Eat that and just relax.

STAN: Thank you, Ollie. (*Sound of munching.*)

OLLIE: Now, let's see where I was . . . Oh, yes. Ladies and gentlemen, this is Oliver Hardy speaking. I'm taking this opportunity of thanking you and the countless friends in the British Isles for the wonderfully warmhearted reception you've given me on my first visit to your beautiful country.

STAN: (*Choking.*) Ollie.

OLLIE: What?

STAN: Speak up.

OLLIE: What for?

STAN: I can't hear you.

OLLIE: Well, if you'll get that egg down you'll be able to hear me much better.

STAN: I just did get the egg down.

OLLIE: What did you do with the eggshell?

STAN: What eggshell?

OLLIE: Don't tell me you've eaten the egg with the *shell* on it?

STAN: Well, I didn't know. You didn't tell me—

OLLIE: Ohhhhh!!

STAN: You don't happen to have another one, do you?

OLLIE: No, I haven't.

STAN: You got any nuts?

OLLIE: (*Indignant.*) No, I haven't got any nuts.

STAN: Well, what did you do with those we bought in New York?

OLLIE: I left them in my wardrobe trunk.

STAN: Where is your trunk? Maybe we can go and get them?

OLLIE: That reminds me. Where is my trunk? I haven't seen it for several days.

STAN: Have you felt in all your pockets?

OLLIE: Now, that's a good idea. I'll take a look and— What do you mean—have I felt in all my pockets? Will you please stop annoying me while I make my speech?

STAN: I'm not annoying you. I'm not doing anything.

OLLIE: Now keep quiet!

STAN: All right.

OLLIE: Ladies and gentlemen—(*Makes his beaming titter of embarrassment.*)

STAN: Stop wiggling your tie.

OLLIE: What do you mean stop wiggling my tie?

STAN: Well, every time you get fancy you start wiggling your tie and it looks silly.

OLLIE: If you interrupt me again, I'll wiggle *you*. (STAN *cries*.) What are you crying for?

STAN: I don't want to be wiggled.

OLLIE: Pardon me, ladies and gentlemen, I wish to speak to my friend privately. (*To* STAN.) What are you trying to do, spoil my speech?

STAN: No, that's impossible.

OLLIE: You bet your *life* it's impossible.

STAN: That's the first time you've agreed with me, Ollie.

OLLIE: Oh, you're getting sarcastic, heh?

STAN: No, I'm not.

OLLIE: Well, just for that *you* make a speech.

STAN: I don't want to make a speech.

OLLIE: Oh yes, you will make a speech.

STAN: I don't know anything about it.

OLLIE: Go ahead.

STAN: All right. Ladies and gentlemen—

OLLIE: (*Snaps finger*) With your *hat* off.

STAN: Oh, I beg your puddin'—ah, pardon. Ladies and gentlemen, with your hat off. I—

OLLIE: You don't say that.

STAN: Oh. Ladies and gentlemen, with*out* your hat off—

OLLIE: Ah, go ahead.

STAN: Ladies and gentlemen, you'll never know how happy we are to be here with you tonight in Chicago, America. It's the first—

OLLIE: Ohhhh!! We're in London, you fool. *London.*

STAN: Well, I didn't know. We've been traveling to so many places, I wasn't quite sure just where we were.

OLLIE: Ah, just go ahead. It won't make any difference anyway.

STAN: So this is London, eh?

OLLIE: Yes, London.

STAN: Ladies and gentlemen, I—

OLLIE: You said that once.

STAN: All right. I'm so happy to be here with you tonight in London, Scotland. I—

OLLIE: That's done it. No more speeches.

STAN: What do you mean, no more speeches? We've got to do something.

OLLIE: All right, maybe I can sing a little song.

STAN: That's a good idea. Oh, say, that reminds me.

OLLIE: What?

STAN: I wish I'd brought my piano with me from America.

OLLIE: You don't have to bring a piano all the way from America. There's plenty here.

STAN: I know, but I wish I'd brought *mine*.

OLLIE: Now, why in your wildest dreams do you wish you'd brought *your* piano with you?

STAN: Well, you won't be mad with me if I tell you, will you?

OLLIE: Oh no, you know I couldn't really get mad with *you!*

STAN: No, I'd rather not tell you. I'd rath—

OLLIE: Oh come on now. Why do you wish that you'd brought *your* piano with you?

STAN: Well, I left our return tickets lying on top of it.

OLLIE: Ohhhh! (STAN *cries.*) Will you shut up? You've done enough damage.

STAN: What damage?

OLLIE: You've left our tickets in America and now we've got to swim back.

STAN: How far is it?

OLLIE: Oh, it's only three thousand miles.

STAN: Well, that's not bad. It's only fifteen hundred miles each!

OLLIE: Ohhhh! (STAN *cries.*)

STAN: (*Happily through the tears.*) Good-bye!

THE WEDDING PARTY (1938)*

(This, the pilot script for a proposed Laurel and Hardy radio series, was recorded before a live audience. Sponsors failed to materialize although several evinced interest. The other characters in the sketch are Patsy Moran (1905–1968) who appeared in several Laurel and Hardy films—she can be seen as

* While the script is dated "1938" in Stan's handwriting, the sketch was broadcast on a 1943 episode of "Mail Call," aired by Armed Forces Radio Service.

Ollie's old girl friend in *Block-Heads*—and Edgar Kennedy (1890–1948) of slow-burn fame whose connection with Laurel and Hardy went all the way back to their silent films.)

OLLIE: Well, the justice of the peace lives right up here, Stanley. Just think. In a few minutes, you and Patsy will be one.

STAN: One what?

OLLIE: One husband and one wife!

STAN: But that makes two.

OLLIE: Oh, shut up.

PATSY: Will you two can that chatter? I want to get this wedding over with.

OLLIE: Do you feel all right, sweetheart?

STAN: I certainly do. I feel fine and—

OLLIE: Not you! It's Patsy I'm talking to. Now come on and let's go. Ouch—my foot! Will you watch where you're going?

STAN: Well, I can't see a thing with this veil on.

OLLIE: *You* don't wear the veil—the bride wears it. Here, put it on, Patsy.

PATSY: Thanks, Ollie.

OLLIE: Did you get some orange blossoms for her hair like I told you to?

STAN: I couldn't find the orange blossoms so I got some oranges instead.

PATSY: Yeah, real oranges—look!

OLLIE: Oh, so that's what's hanging in front of your eyes?

PATSY: Yes.

OLLIE: How do you keep them there?

STAN: She's got *bags* for them.

OLLIE: Will you keep still? Now let's go in to the justice of the peace.

STAN: Ollie.

OLLIE: What?

STAN: I'm scared.

OLLIE: Scared of what?

STAN: Well, I'm going to marry Patsy, and we've only been going steady for twelve years, and I'm kind of scared.

OLLIE: Now, don't be nervous. Take a little shot of this.

STAN: What is it?

OLLIE: Sixteen-year-old prune punch. It'll bolster you right up. Here.

(SOUND: *gurgling gullet.*)

STAN: Thank you, Ollie. Oh, boy—that's good. Thank you, Ollie. Here's the bottle.

OLLIE: Where's the cork?

STAN: What cork?

OLLIE: The cork that was in the bottle.

STAN: Oh, I thought that was a prune pit, and I swallowed it.

PATSY: Say, will you please ring the bell and stop wasting my time?

STAN: O.K.

(SOUND: *bell.*)

OLLIE: Ring it louder. We've got to wake the justice up.

STAN: What's the matter. Is he dead?

OLLIE: Ohhh! Here, I'll ring it.

(SOUND: *bell.*)

That's the way to do it!

(SOUND: *water being poured over* OLLIE *from above.*)

Ohhh!

STAN: What happened?

EDGAR: What's going on here? What's all the racket?

PATSY: We'd like to get married if it's not too much trouble.

EDGAR: Not too much trouble? Getting a guy up at this time of the night!

STAN: What are *you* squawking about? *We're* up! (*Hiccups.*)

PATSY: The court's up too. *

OLLIE: Now I can take my finger out of this bottle.

EDGAR: Well, as long as I'm up, come in. (*Pause.*) Well, are you coming in or not?

ALL: Sure . . . Yes, we're coming . . . Oh, yes.

(SOUND: *entering the house.*)

EDGAR: Now, which is which here?

OLLIE: Well, this is she, and that's *it!* (STAN *makes indignant noises at being so described.*)

EDGAR: My goodness, young lady, where did you get that veil you're wearing?

PATSY: From my father.

---

* The line is actually, "The cork's up, too!" (Stan's hiccup is followed by a "pop" sound effect — he's just ejected the cork he swallowed.)

OLLIE: He keeps bees, Judge.

EDGAR: Oh. (*To* STAN.) Young man, you're very lucky to have a girl like this. (*To* PATSY.) Umm, my dear, you have lovely orange eyes.

PATSY: Thank you, Judge. Have one?

EDGAR: No, thank you.

STAN: I'll have one if you don't mind.

OLLIE: You can eat later.

EDGAR: Now, miss, we'll have to fill out this certificate. What's your name, please?

PATSY: Patsy Moran.

EDGAR: What?

OLLIE: Moran. M-o-r-o-n.

    (SOUND: JUDGE *hitting* OLLIE *in the eye;* OLLIE *reacting.*)

EDGAR: You keep out of this. Now, what's *your* name?

STAN: My name? Laurel. But call me Stanley for short.

EDGAR: And where were you born?

STAN: Born? Bridge, Minnesota.

EDGAR: Bridge?

STAN: Yes, right on the bridge between St. Paul, and Minneapolis. You know, I'll never forget that morning. All the cows were coming around and there was such— *

EDGAR: Will you keep quiet? All right now. Stand here before me.

    (SOUND: STAN *hiccups.*)

STAN: Excuse me.

---

* The line should read, "All the cars were coming around, and there were trucks coming around…"

EDGAR: Well, let's go. I want to get back to bed. Now, young lady, do you take this man to be your lawfully wedded husband?

PATSY: I do.

EDGAR: And you, Stanley-for-short. Do you take this woman to be your lawfully wedded wife?

STAN: I—ah, I don't think so.

EDGAR: Why not?

STAN: I've taken a dislike to her.

OLLIE: (*Incredulous.*) You've taken a *dislike* to her?

STAN: Yep. (SOUND: PATSY *crying, then fainting.*)

OLLIE: Quick, Judge. She's fainted.

STAN: Get her some brandy.

EDGAR: I haven't got any brandy.

PATSY: (*Quickly.*) A beer'll do.

STAN: You're a fine judge. No brandy! Huh!

EDGAR: Now, just a minute, just a minute. Did you or did you not wake me up out of a sound sleep to marry you?

STAN: I don't remember. (*Hiccups.*)

EDGAR: And now you stand there and say you don't want to go through with it?

STAN: Well, I'm sorry. I changed my mind. I couldn't help it.

EDGAR: (*Yells.*) Why, you little—

OLLIE: Come on, Patsy. Let's get out of here.

(SOUND: *party leaving for outside.*)

PATSY: (*Crying.*) Oh, Stanley, you brute.

STAN: I can't help it, Patsy. I just—

OLLIE: Stanley.

STAN: What, Ollie?

OLLIE: You came out here to get married, didn't you?

STAN: Yes.

OLLIE: You took poor little Patsy away from her mother—
her home.

STAN: Yes, I know but—

OLLIE: You stood her up at the altar. Only a cad would do
that.

STAN: (*Cries.*) I'm sorry. I—

OLLIE: Now we're going back in there and you're going to
behave yourself.

STAN: Ollie.

OLLIE: What?

STAN: Give me another shot.

OLLIE: (*Disgustedly.*) Oh, here.

(SOUND: *gurgling gullet.*)

STAN: Oh, that's good, thank you.

OLLIE: Now kiss and make up.

(SOUND: *large suction effect.*)

Oh, not *me! Patsy!*

(SOUND: *bell.*)

EDGAR: Oh, so it's you again, eh?

OLLIE: Now everything's straightened out, Judge. I've talked
to Stanley.

EDGAR: It better be. Come in. Now stand before me. Young man, do you take this woman to be your lawful wedded wife?

STAN: I do.

EDGAR: Fine. Now, young woman, do you take this man to be your lawful wedded husband?

PATSY: I should say not. I've taken a dislike to him.

STAN: Well, can you beat that?

EDGAR: Why, you two little whippersnappers, I'll take the both of you and wring your necks.

OLLIE: Come on, come on. Let's get out of here.

(SOUND: *party leaving for outside.*)

This is another fine mess you've gotten me into. Now look Patsy, you came out here to get married, didn't you?

PATSY: Sure.

OLLIE: You took poor little Stanley away from me. You broke up *my* home. You brought him all the way here to Las Vegas.

PATSY: (*Tearfully.*) Yes, I know.

OLLIE: And when you get here, you leave him standing at the altar. You ought to be ashamed of yourself.

PATSY: Oh, I'm sorry.

OLLIE: Now, kiss and make up.

(SOUND: *large suction effect.*)

Not *me!* Stanley! Now come on, let's go in.

STAN: Ollie.

OLLIE: What is it *now?*

STAN: What about another shot?

OLLIE: Not now.

PATSY: Make it two.

OLLIE: Wait until after you're married.

    (SOUND: *bell.*)

STAN: (*To* JUDGE.) Surprise!

EDGAR: Surprise? Why, you—

OLLIE: Oh, calm down, Judge. Now everything is all settled.

EDGAR: Oh, it is, eh? Step right in, folks.

PATSY: Thank you, Judge.

EDGAR: Now stand before me. Do you take this man to be your lawful wedded husband?

PATSY: I do.

EDGAR: And do you take this woman to be your lawful wedded wife?

STAN: I do.

EDGAR: Well, I won't marry you!

OLLIE: Why not?

EDGAR: Because I've taken a dislike to the whole *bunch* of you!

OLLIE: But, Judge—

EDGAR: Get out of here!

    (SOUND: *party leaving.*)

PATSY: Well, it looks like back to the laundry for me.

STAN: Ollie, what about that shot you promised me?

OLLIE: (*Sweetly.*) Oh, thank you, Stanley. I'm glad you reminded me. *Here* it is!!

(SOUND: *gunshot. Into theme, "The Dance of the Cuckoos."*)

THE DRIVERS' LICENSE SKETCH (1939–47)

(Stan first wrote the sketch for performance at a Red Cross benefit during the 1939 San Francisco World's Fair. When Laurel and Hardy went on their 1947 tour of the English music halls, another character was added and the sketch was expanded by about five minutes. It is the final script which is printed here.)

(*In one.* [In front of stage curtain.] STAN *and* OLLIE *stand in front of microphone.* STAN *seems very unhappy.*)

OLLIE: Good evening, ladies and gentlemen—

STAN: Can I say something?

OLLIE: (*Glaring.*) No, you cannot. Can't you see I'm speaking to the ladies and gentlemen? (*To audience, smiling.*) As I was saying—good evening, ladies and gentlemen! It's a very real pleasure for Stan and me to be here with you tonight—

STAN: Say, can I say something?

OLLIE: What is it *now?* Will you pardon me a moment, ladies and gentlemen? My friend, Mr. Laurel, has something to tell me. Now then, Stanley, what is it?

Preparing for a BBC radio broadcast, London, 1932.

James Parrott, Charles Rogers and Felix Adler join Stan in a script conference.

Jane Pickens (top), John Garfield, Ray Bolger, Mitzi Mayfair, Babe, Stan and Chico Marx on USO tour, 1941.

Stan receives his "wings" for participating in Carribean USO tour, 1941.

Performing the "Driver's License Sketch" on tour in
England, 1947.

Backstage at the Hippodrome during "Birds of a Feather," Birmingham, 1953. *Photo by Robert Fusillo.*

STAN: You're standing on my foot! (OLLIE *tie-twiddles to the audience.*)

OLLIE: I beg your pardon, I'm sure. And now, ladies and gentlemen, if you don't mind—Stanley would like to say a few words to you. Come, Stanley.

STAN: What'll I say?

OLLIE: Just say, hello everybody! (*Irritated.*) But with your hat off!

STAN: Hello, everybody—but with your hat off!

OLLIE: Ohhhh!

STAN: What will I say?

OLLIE: Just make a nice, long speech.

STAN: But we haven't got time.

OLLIE: What d'ye mean, we haven't got time?

STAN: Well, we've got to get our new driver's licenses. You know the old one perspires tomorrow.

OLLIE: Oh, what ignorance! You mean *transpire.* But for once, ladies and gentlemen, Stan is right. We do have to get our new drivers' licenses. Come, Stanley. (*They walk into the set in two.*)

(*In two. Behind the stage curtain, we find the following: a typical traffic bureau, with a desk center and behind it a swivel chair in which sits a police officer. Left of the desk a straight chair. At rise, the cop is busy looking through the lower right drawer in desk.* STAN *and* OLLIE *enter with the "you-after-me, Stanley" business, the cop not noticing them. Finally,* OLLIE, *with a big flourish, rings the bell on the desk.*)

COP: (*Surprised.*) Good morning, gentlemen. What can I do for you?

OLLIE: Excuse me, just a moment. (OLLIE *takes his walking stick off his arm, sticks it into the stage where it stays. He then removes his hat and places it on top of the cane.* OLLIE *then brings out a sling that is hanging around his neck, places his right arm in it, then tie-twiddles to the* COP.)

COP: Well, what can I do for you?

OLLIE: If you don't mind, I'd like to renew my driver's license.

COP: (*Picks out an application form and hands to* OLLIE.) Just fill out the application.

OLLIE: I'm sorry, sir, but owing to a slight accident, I don't write.

COP: Well, get your friend to fill it in for you.

OLLIE: I'm sorry, sir, but you see, he can write but he can't read.

COP: If you can't write and he can't read, how come?

STAN: Well, you see, we both went to different schools together.

COP: (*To* OLLIE.) What happened to your arm?

OLLIE: Well, you see, sir, it was like this. We were driving down Main Street, not paying any attention to anything.

COP: (*Sarcastically.*) You say you were driving in heavy traffic, not paying any attention to anything?

STAN: Yes. That was the day you fell asleep. Remember, Ollie?

OLLIE: (*All smiles.*) Yes, that's right, Stanley.

COP: Then what happened?

OLLIE: Well, I suddenly awakened and realized that I had to make a left-hand turn, so naturally I stuck out my right hand.

COP: Oh. You were going to make a left-hand turn so you stuck out your right hand?

STAN: Yes sir. Just like that. (STAN *has a removable cotton-wrapped splint on the first finger of his right hand, and as he motions, sticking out his right hand, the finger splint flies offstage. He realizes what has happened, and he and* OLLIE *start to look for it.* OLLIE *looks in wastepaper basket, etc.*)

STAN: Never mind, Ollie. I have a spare. (*He brings another one out of his pocket and sticks it on his finger. The cop is getting a bit annoyed.* OLLIE *indignantly pushes* STAN.)

OLLIE: Sit down. (STAN *sits down in the chair.*)

COP: Then what happened?

OLLIE: Well, when I came out of the hospital—

COP: Were you in the hospital?

OLLIE: (*Showing his arm in the sling.*) Oh, yes.

STAN: Show him the picture, Ollie.

COP: What? Have you got a picture?

OLLIE: Oh, yes. (*Reaches in his pocket and brings out a picture postcard which he hands to the cop.* OLLIE *points to it.*) That's me in the end bed.

Cop: Now, just a minute. There is nobody in that end bed. (OLLIE *does a take, looks closely at the picture.* STAN *comes over and looks at the picture.*)

STAN: I can explain that.

Cop: How?

STAN: Well, you see, I had to leave the room for a few minutes when I was taking that picture.

Cop: (*Does big double-take, then gets irritated.*) Well, you can't write, and he can't read. What are we going to do about it?

OLLIE: (*Twiddles his tie.*) I thought that maybe, sir, *you* would be kind enough to fill it out for me.

Cop: As a rule I don't do this sort of thing, but under the circumstances, I'll break the rule.

OLLIE: Oh, thank you.

STAN: That's very kind of you. We sure appreciate it. (*Hands cop a ruler.*)

OLLIE: (*Angrily.*) He doesn't mean *that* kind of rule.

Cop: All right. (*To* OLLIE.) What is your name?

OLLIE: Oliver N. Hardy. And this is my good friend, Mr. Laurel. (*As he turns to introduce* STAN *to the cop,* STAN *has already walked in front of* OLLIE. OLLIE *is looking for* STAN *as* STAN *actually begins to shake hands with the cop. The cop has put down his pen to shake with* STAN, *and as* STAN *finishes shaking hands with him, his finger splint is left on the cop's hands. The cop, not realizing, uses the splint as a pen. He dips it in the ink well and prepares to write again, then suddenly realizes what has happened. Very disgustedly, he throws the finger splint into the wastepaper basket.* STAN *puts out yet another finger splint and puts it on his own finger.*)

COP: Now then, back to business. (*To* OLLIE.) You say your name is Oliver N. Hardy?

OLLIE: That's correct, sir.

COP: What does the N. stand for?

OLLIE: *Enry.*

COP: *Enry?*

STAN: Yes, *Enry Ardy.*

COP: Enry Ardy?

STAN: Yes. And you spell the Holiver with a "Ho"!

COP: Enry? Now see here, you do *not* write Henry with an N.

STAN: (*Indignantly.*) Of course you don't. You write it with a pencil!

OLLIE: (*Pushes* STAN *back in chair.*) Why don't you do something to *help* me? I'll never get my license.

COP: (*To* OLLIE.) What's your address?

OLLIE: We *used* to live at 254 South Main Street. But that was before we moved.

COP: What did you move for?

OLLIE: Well, you see, sir—we couldn't get the landlord to raise our rent.

COP: (*Amazed.*) What on earth did you want the landlord to raise your rent for?

STAN: Well, *we* couldn't raise it, could we, Ollie?

OLLIE: No, sir.

COP: Listen to me very carefully, you. Have you ever been apprehended for contravening a traffic regulation? (OLLIE *does big take*, STAN *unglues eyes and scratches head.*)

OLLIE: I beg your pardon?

COP: Have you ever been *arrested* for *breaking* the traffic laws?

OLLIE: Oh, yes sir. For speeding once.

COP: Speeding? How fast were you going?

OLLIE: Ten miles an hour.

COP: Ten miles an hour? That's not speeding, my dear boy. You can go ten miles an hour any place.

STAN: Not on the sidewalk, could you, Ollie?

COP: I've had enough of this. Let me see your old driver's license.

OLLIE: Yes, sir. (*He starts to feel in his pockets.*) Help me find it, Stanley. (STAN *helps him search for it but the finger splint gets in the way, so* STAN *puts the finger splint on one of* OLLIE's *fingers while he goes through his pockets for him.* STAN *finds the driver's license and hands it to the cop. He then takes back the finger splint from* OLLIE's *finger and in doing so jerks it a little hard, which causes* OLLIE's *hand to fly back and hit the cop in the face, knocking the cop's hat off.* OLLIE, *full of apologies, picks the cop's hat up and in his excitement puts it back on the cop's head, back to front.*)

OLLIE: I'm awfully sorry, sir.

COP: (*Feeling his nose.*) Well, don't let it happen again.

OLLIE: (*Full of apology.*) No, sir. (*Cop realizes his hat is on back to front, straightens it and composes himself.*)

COP: Now, where did you get your old driver's license?

OLLIE: It was left to me by my grandfather.

COP: (*Taking it big.*) Just a minute. Who told you you could drive a car with your grandfather's license?

STAN: I did. Didn't I, Ollie?

OLLIE: (*All smiles.*) That's right, Stan.

COP: Is that so? Well, we'll just find out how much you know about driving your grandfather's car. (*He gets out of his chair to give an examination to* OLLIE.) Now then. Over here is a curbstone, a portion of it is painted red. What does that mean?

OLLIE: (*Very confident.*) That means there's no parking.

COP: How do you know it means no parking?

STAN: Well, it says so. Anybody can read it.

COP: Just a minute, just a minute. I thought you told me you couldn't read?

STAN: Oh, I can read reading but I can't read writing.

COP: (*Burns up.*) Oh, you can read reading, can you?

STAN: Yes, sir.

COP: (*Hands* STAN *an application form.*) Well, read that!

STAN: (*Takes the form, looks puzzled, studies it for a second.*) Oh, I can't read *that* reading.

COP: Why?

STAN: Well, it's too close to the paper.

COP: Too close to the paper?

STAN: Now you give me a question.

COP: I'll give you a punch in the nose if you don't keep quiet. (*Points to* OLLIE.) Now *you*. Getting back to your grandfather's car. You're on top of a hill and you're coming down that hill at sixty miles an hour.

STAN: What? In his grandfather's car?

COP: Yes, in his grandfather's car.

STAN: But we've got no brakes.

COP: Nevertheless, you're coming down the hill at sixty miles an hour. (STAN, *getting very interested, sits down in the cop's chair at the desk*.) Now, you throw it into first gear, and it won't work. You throw it into second gear— and it won't work. Finally, you throw it into *third* gear, and *still* it won't work. (*Cop takes off hat in the excitement*.)

STAN: Why don't you throw in his grandfather? He won't work either!

OLLIE: (*To* STAN.) You better be careful. You're going to get into his hair. (*Cop has a bald head and suddenly realizes what* OLLIE *has said. Puts hat back on quickly*.)

COP: Now, at the bottom of the hill is a railroad crossing. Coming from the left is an express train thundering along the tracks at eighty miles an hour. Smoke and flames are belching from the smokestack. The engineer is covered with grease, dirt and grime. He is blinded by smoke. He can't even see to reach down and grab the emergency throttle. Then—coming from the right—is an ambulance tearing along the highway at ninety miles an hour. It's an emergency case and life is at stake. The siren is screaming, "Clear the way! Clear the way!" Nothing must stand in the way of progress, and little does the engineer or the driver of the ambulance know that your grandfather's car is coming down the hill at sixty miles an hour!

(During this speech, STAN and OLLIE have found the cop's lunch box. The cop is so excited by the dramatics in his speech that he pays attention only to what he is saying. STAN opens the lunch box, finds an apple which he gives to OLLIE, finds a banana which he puts in his pocket, finds a cigar which he is about to put in his mouth. OLLIE taps him on the shoulder. STAN says "Sorry" and starts to hand OLLIE the cigar. OLLIE, by mistake, instead of taking the cigar takes STAN's finger splint and puts it in his mouth. Suddenly realizes what he's doing. STAN takes the finger splint back, puts it on his finger again, and looks in the lunch box once more. Here he finds some crackers, hands some to OLLIE and both commence to eat the crackers while the cop is raving about the train and ambulance. They haven't paid any attention to what the cop has been saying. The cop by now has worn himself out with his description. At the end of his speech, he slams the desk and says, "Now"—which scares STAN and OLLIE, and they spit crackers all over the stage.)

COP: So then—which would you hit—the ambulance, or the train?

OLLIE (*Looking at* STAN, *who is equally baffled.* OLLIE *whispers to* STAN): Did you hear what he said? (*Cop meanwhile takes up a pitcher of water, pours out a glass and starts to drink.*) Pardon me, sir. My friend is a little confused. Would you mind going through all that again?

COP: (*Spits out all the water. He is flabbergasted but says weakly*): All right. (STAN *and* OLLIE *are now going to pay close attention. Cop starts all over again.*) You're on top of a hill.

STAN: (*Whispering to* OLLIE.) We're on top of a hill.

COP: (*Enraged. Swings* STAN *around in his chair.*) Listen, I'm not talking to you. You're not in it. Do you understand? You're not in it.

STAN: I am too, aren't I, Ollie?

COP: (*Angrily pushing* STAN *out of his chair.*) And you are not in my seat, either.

OLLIE: (*Pushing* STAN *indignantly into the other chair.*) You're not in it. Don't you understand? Now sit down. (STAN *cries.*)

STAN: Always picking on me! I try to do everything I can. (*He turns suddenly and sees* OLLIE *glaring at him, so goes back to the dead pan. The cop, in the meantime, has sat down in his own chair.* OLLIE *turns to him, moves the cop out of his chair, and sits himself down in it.*)

OLLIE: Now, what were you saying, officer?

COP: (*Weakened now by the whole thing, starts his speech all over again, very wearily.*) You're at the top of a hill. You're coming down the hill at sixty miles an hour—

(*As he starts to speak,* STAN *brings the banana out of his pocket, peels it, takes a bite of it, and then starts to eat. On his second bite, he mistakes the banana for his finger splint, bites off the end of the finger splint and enjoys it every bit as much as he did the banana.* OLLIE *and the cop have stopped talking and center their gaze on* STAN. STAN *after several bites realizes it doesn't taste quite the same as the banana, and has great difficulty in swallowing the cotton off the finger splint.* STAN *suddenly realizes the situation and looks at* OLLIE.)

OLLIE: (*Very annoyed.*) Throw that thing away. What do you think this is—a lunchroom? (OLLIE *then looks at the cop and says,* "Proceed." *At the same time, he takes the apple out of his pocket and takes a big bite out of it. The cop goes into his story once again, goes through it with all the same melodramatics, and at the end repeats*):

COP: And so, which one would you hit—the ambulance or the train?

OLLIE: I'd hit the train.

COP: Oh, you would, would you?

STAN: That's right, the train!

COP: And why would you blithering idiots hit the train?

STAN: (*Triumphantly.*) Well, we'd need the ambulance to get home in!

COP: Now just for that, you don't get your driver's license.

OLLIE: Why not?

COP: Because you are *not* supposed to be going sixty miles an hour coming down that hill!

OLLIE: (*Indignant.*) Give me back my old license. You just wait until my grandfather hears about this.

COP: (*This is too much.*) You get out of here! (OLLIE *gives him the apple core, and cop takes shotgun from behind desk and blasts away as the boys run out. Cop trips on* OLLIE's *cane and shoots in the air.*)

OLLIE: Why don't you watch where you're shooting?

BLACKOUT

BIRDS OF A FEATHER (1953)

(This sketch Stan wrote for Laurel and Hardy's last tour of the British music halls, and—as it happened—for their last professional appearance together anywhere.)

(*Scene one: a street, in one. Stan and Ollie enter, going in different directions. They meet center, nod, say "how do you do" as they pass each other. Then both do big double-take.*)

OLLIE: I thought you were going to meet me here at ten-thirty?

STAN: (*Looks at watch.*) I am. (*Starts to leave.*)

OLLIE: Where are you going?

STAN: I'm too early. It's only a quarter to.

114

OLLIE: Come back, let me look at that. (*Looks at* STAN's *watch.*) It's stopped.

STAN: What time is it?

OLLIE: (*Looks at own watch.*) Exactly ten-thirty. Why can't you be prompt? Where have you been?

STAN: I was just talking to a feller down the street and he told me where we could get a job.

OLLIE: What kind of job?

STAN: At a distillery.

OLLIE: What doing?

STAN: As whiskey tasters.

OLLIE: Whiskey tasters! Did you get all the details?

STAN: Sure.

OLLIE: What do we have to do?

STAN: We have to keep tasting whiskey until we get the proof.

OLLIE: Proof of what?

STAN: Whether it's a single or a double.

OLLIE: That sounds interesting. Did he give you any qualifications we'd have to have to get the job?

STAN: Oh, sure. The first thing they want to know is—are you willing?

OLLIE: Well, I'd be willing. How about you?

STAN: I'm willing if you are.

OLLIE: Well, if that's all there is to it, we'll take it.

STAN: Yeah—and they pay good money too.

OLLIE: You mean they pay money as well?

STAN: Sure, we work on commission.

OLLIE: How do you mean?

STAN: The more you drink, the more you earn.

OLLIE: The more you drink the more you earn?

STAN: Sure, and you get paid double for overtime.

OLLIE: Well, what are we waiting for?

STAN: I don't know.

OLLIE: Come on, the more we drink—the more we earn.

(They exit to music. Scene two. Tabs open, revealing a hospital room. OLLIE discovered propped up in bed, partly dressed. He has an ice pack on his head, one arm in a sling. It is a small single bed to make OLLIE look uncomfortable. On the left of the set is a heavy door. Center is the bed. On the right is a practical window. Left of center is a three-way screen with lettering across the top reading, "Mental Ward —County Hospital." A small lightweight metal wastebasket behind the screen. Also a nightstand, trick cabinet and chair. A knock is heard at door.)

OLLIE: Come in. *(Door opens into room revealing sign hanging on outside of door which says "Mental Case— No Visitors." Also on the door we see oversized bolt for barring door from outside. STAN enters, carrying paper bag and lilies.)*

STAN: Hi. How do you feel?

OLLIE: Never mind how I feel. What took you so long to get here?

STAN: The hospital foreman wouldn't let me in. He said "No visitors."

OLLIE: Well, how did you manage?

STAN: Simple. I told them I was a relative. I told him I was your son. And it worked like a charm.

OLLIE: My son! You have a lot of nerve telling them I was your father.

STAN: I couldn't tell them you were my mother.

OLLIE: Of course you couldn't. I've never even been married.

STAN: Gee, I never thought of that.

OLLIE: You *wouldn't*.

STAN: Oh, well—come easy—go easy. Look what I brought you. (*Opens paper bag.*)

OLLIE: Never mind that. What am I doing here?

STAN: Didn't you hear? You're a menthol case.

OLLIE: Menthol case! What's that?

STAN: It means you're balmy.

OLLIE: Balmy?

STAN: Sure. You jumped out of a top-floor window.

OLLIE: Who, me? When?

STAN: This morning. You remember, we went to a distillery to get a job.

OLLIE: Sure, to try out as whiskey tasters.

STAN: Well, after tasting all morning, we were so willing,

the fellow gave us the job, and you were so pleased you had a couple of doubles to celebrate.

OLLIE: A couple of doubles?

STAN: Yeah—I think it was three doubles you had.

OLLIE: After drinking all morning.

STAN: Yes—and then you said you felt as happy as a lark, and thought you'd like to fly around with the birds for a while.

OLLIE: Fly around with the birds?

STAN: Sure. Then you opened the window and out you went. I can see you now—flapping your arms just like a cuckoo.

OLLIE: Well, why didn't you *stop* me?

STAN: Well, I was celebrating too—and I thought you could *do* it.

OLLIE: Why, it's a miracle I'm alive.

STAN: It sure is. Lucky you fell in the river.

OLLIE: Fell in the river? Why, I might have drowned. I can't swim a stroke.

STAN: I know it. That's why I ran home by bus, and called the police.

OLLIE: Do you mean to tell me that while I was drowning, you wasted time getting a *bus*?

STAN: Well, I couldn't get a taxi. I waited half an hour for one. Then I tried to hitch a ride—and *then* I got a bus. What's wrong with a bus? You were saved, weren't you?

OLLIE: Yes, but it might have been too late.

STAN: That's what I figured. Better late than never.

OLLIE: Well, how did I get here?

STAN: The police brought you. They knew they were going to arrest you at first.

OLLIE: Arrest me? For what?

STAN: For drunk flying.

OLLIE: Ridiculous.

STAN: That's what I told them. I gave them a piece of my mind.

OLLIE: What did they say to *that?*

STAN: I don't know. When I woke up you were all gone.

OLLIE: (*Notices the lilies.*) What are the flowers for?

STAN: Well, I thought you broke your neck—and I didn't want to come emptyhanded. Besides I always knew you liked chrysanthemum-mum-mum-mums.

OLLIE: Where did you get the money to pay for them?

STAN: Well, that was your overtime at the distillery. You see, I'm still working. I'm willing. (*Gives flowers.*) Here.

OLLIE: (*Pushing flowers away.*) Oh, put them away somewhere.

STAN: What will I do with them?

OLLIE: Oh, I don't care. Find something to put them in. (STAN *looks around for place to put flowers. Hands flowers to* OLLIE, *looks in cabinet, then under bed. Finds lightweight basket behind screen, brings it out and takes flowers from* OLLIE. OLLIE *watches him dur-*

ing this, exasperated. STAN *places flowers in wastebasket, sets them up on shelf over bed.*)

OLLIE: What's in the bag? (STAN *opens paper bag, takes out sandwich.*)

STAN: Your favorite—a nice onion and jam sandwich.

OLLIE: I can't eat that.

STAN: You always said you liked jam—and you liked onions, too.

OLLIE: I do, but not together.

STAN: What's the difference? Come on—try it.

OLLIE: I don't want to, I tell you.

STAN: (*Trying to coax him.*) Come on, it'll do you good. (*Threatening.*) I'll give it to the doctor.

OLLIE: I don't care *who* you give it to.

STAN: (*Reaches in pocket, brings out two eggs.*) How about a couple of nice, fresh eggs? They're still warm. You can get some milk—

OLLIE: I told you I don't want *anything.*

STAN: (*Puts eggs on night stand near table.*) Well, I just thought you'd like some hog-neg.
(*Door opens and nurse enters, named* ROSIE PARKER. *She is carrying a pair of pajamas, towel, and chart.*)

NURSE: (*To* OLLIE.) Good afternoon, and how's my little dickey bird?

OLLIE: What do you mean, little dickey bird?

STAN: She's nuts!

NURSE: (*Screams when she sees* STAN.) What's that?

OLLIE: This is my good friend, Mr. Laurel.

STAN: How do you do?

OLLIE: (*Snaps fingers at* STAN.) The hat! (STAN *doesn't understand. Looks at nurse's cap and then at* OLLIE.) Take it off! (STAN *reaches over and takes nurse's cap off.* OLLIE *grabs* STAN's *hat off. Hat mix-up routine.*)

NURSE: And what are you doing here, may I ask?

STAN: I just popped in to see him.

NURSE: Well, just pop out. No visitors are allowed.

STAN: You can't put me out. I'm a relative. (*To* OLLIE.) Aren't I?

OLLIE: That's right.

STAN: That's right. I'm his son, and he's not married.

NURSE: (*To* OLLIE.) I thought you said he was a friend.

OLLIE: He *is* a friend. A friendly relative.

NURSE: That explains everything. You look like you were hatched.

OLLIE: Never mind what he looks like. What's that chart say?

NURSE: (*Reads chart.*) "For the attention of Dr. Berserk. Patient thinks he's a bird. Advise immediate frontal lobotomy and dissection of the cerebellum."

STAN: What's that?

NURSE: Dissection of the cerebellum?

OLLIE: What does that mean?

NURSE: It means sawing open your cranium and taking out

your brains for observation. (STAN *and* OLLIE *take this big.*)

OLLIE: Not my cranium!

NURSE: Now, don't worry about Dr. Berserk. He's a positive wizard with a knife. His operations are always successful even if the patient dies.

STAN: Oh, well—that's different.

OLLIE: What's different about it?

STAN: Well, if you don't die, you have nothing to worry about. You still have your geranium.

NURSE: (*To* STAN.) Are you sure you just dropped in to *visit?*

STAN: I didn't drop in; I popped in. P-o-opped in.

NURSE: (*To* STAN.) Oh, never mind. (*To* OLLIE.) Now you put on these pajamas. Dr. Berserk is going to examine you before he operates. (*The pajamas are little boy size.*)

STAN: (*Measuring* OLLIE *with the pajamas.*) They won't fit him.

NURSE: Who cares? He's not going anywhere.

STAN: I know. But what if he walks in his sleep?

NURSE: (*To* OLLIE.) Well, if you need anything, just ring. Ask for Rosie. Rosie Parker. (*Starts out, turns back to* STAN.) And you be careful. This birdie might think you're a worm and gobble you up. (*She exits, singing* "Only a Bird in a Gilded Cage.")

STAN: (*Worried.*) Would you do that?

OLLIE: Do what?

STAN: What she said—gobble me up.

OLLIE: Haven't I got enough troubles of my own without gobbling you up? Gobble you up! What next?

(MUSIC CUE: "Death of Cock Robin." *Enter a character made up like the caricature of an undertaker—dead white face, wearing a high hat with black band, frock coat, white cotton gloves, looking the picture of death itself. He walks slowly to the bed, takes out a tape measure, measures* OLLIE, *width and depth, and marks the figures down in a little notebook. As he starts to turn away, he notices the lilies which he rearranges, after which he gives* OLLIE *an icy stare. He then removes his hat, holds it across his chest, and starts toward the door. He is just about to exit when he suddenly sees* STAN, *gets a thought, takes out the tape measure, and measures* STAN, *repeating the business of marking down in notebook. He exits very slowly.*)

OLLIE: (*Jumps out of bed.*) That's done it. I'm getting out of here.

STAN: Aren't you going to wait for your fitting?

OLLIE: No, not that kind of fitting. And I'm not going to stay here to be operated on.

STAN: I don't blame you.

OLLIE: (*Starts toward door.*) Come on, let's go.

STAN: You can't get out of here. It's locked. Besides, you might run into Nosie. Nosie Parker.

OLLIE: Not Nosie—Rosie!

STAN: Oh—how about the window?

OLLIE: That's a good idea. (*Runs to window, looks down.*) It's a long way down, but we'll take a chance. (*Grabs sheet off bed.*) Quick, help me with these sheets. Tie them together.

STAN: What are you going to do?

OLLIE: We'll lower ourselves out the window.

STAN: That's a good idea. (*They tie two sheets together.* OLLIE *starts one end around his waist, hands other end to* STAN.)

OLLIE: Tie that to something solid. (STAN *looks around, doesn't see anything and finally ties it around his own neck.* OLLIE, *busy, doesn't see this.*) We all ready?

STAN: O.K.

OLLIE: Now, take it easy. (OLLIE *starts climbing out the window, turns, sees* STAN *with sheet tied around neck. Takes it big.*) What are you trying to do, kill me? (*Climbs back in.*) I told you to tie it on to something solid—not around yourself.

STAN: Well, I thought we'd save time by going together. How about me going first?

OLLIE: How do you expect *me* to get out?

STAN: Same way as you did before.

OLLIE: How?

STAN: Fly!

OLLIE: Ohhhh! (*Sudden idea.*) *I know!* Why didn't I think of it before?

STAN: (*As he unties sheet from neck.*) What?

OLLIE: You can go and get me a barrister.

STAN: How'm I going to get out?

OLLIE: (*Indicating door.*) Just stand over there, back of the door.

STAN: Why?

OLLIE: I'll ring for Rosie. When she opens the door, you dash out behind her back.

STAN: What for?

OLLIE: Then you can go and get the barrister.

STAN: What kind?

OLLIE: Any kind. Get me out of here. (OLLIE *rings bell, gathers sheets which are still tied to his waist, pulls them around him as he quickly gets back in bed.*)

STAN: (*Crosses over to him.*) What are you going to bed for?

OLLIE: So Rosie won't get suspicious. You know how nosy Rosie is. Now, quick—before she gets here. (STAN *starts to climb into bed with* OLLIE *who pushes him out.*) No —over there! You want to spoil everything? (STAN *goes to wrong side of the door.*) No—the other side. (STAN *gets in place just as the* NURSE *enters. He exits behind her back.* NURSE *crosses over to bed.*)

NURSE: Now, what do you want? (*Looks around for* STAN.) Where is your friendly offspring?

OLLIE: (*Gets out of bed.*) For your information, madam, he went to get me a barrister.

NURSE: A barrister?

OLLIE: I'll show you and this Dr. Berserk guy. I'll sue everybody in this hospital.

NURSE: Now, now, don't get excited.

OLLIE: Excited? (*Starts to pace, trailing sheet after him.*) You've ruined my career, my good name, you've made a monkey out of me, branding me as a bird—exposed me to the whole world as potty—p-o-otty—*potty!* You just wait until my barrister hears of this. (STAN *enters, holding an object not seen by audience.*)

OLLIE: Ah, just in the nick of time!

STAN: Here! (*Holds out broken-off piece of bannister.*)

OLLIE: What's that?

STAN: A bannister!

OLLIE: You idiot!

NURSE: Hunnhhh! (*Sarcastically.*) Wait until your barrister hears of *this!* You're both nuts! (*She exits, closing door.*)

STAN: (*Still befuddled.*) What do you want me to do with this?

OLLIE: Don't ask me. (*Exasperated, gets back in bed.*) A *bannister!*

STAN: Well, it was the best I could do when nobody was looking.

OLLIE: Sit down. You're always doing something to *upset* me. Can't you ever do anything right?

STAN: What's wrong now?

OLLIE: Every time I ask you to do something, you always mess it up. From now on, when I ask you to do something for me, *don't do it.*

STAN: (*Sits down, trying to figure that out.*) Suppose you don't *ask* me to do something?

OLLIE: Just use your own judgment, think twice, and then count to ten. (*Pause.*) In your case, make it five. (STAN *thinks for a minute, and starts toward nightstand.*) Now what are you trying to do?

STAN: Just exactly what you told me to do. Use my own judgment.

OLLIE: Well, it's about time you used your own head instead of mine. (STAN *picks up water jug on nightstand, reaches for glass on shelf above and knocks the wastebasket of flowers on to* OLLIE's *head.* OLLIE *lets out a yell,* STAN *pours water from jug over* OLLIE, OLLIE *jumps to his feet, shaking off lilies and water. Door opens and* NURSE *ushers* DR. BERSERK *in. He is an eccentric type, dressed in cutaway coat, loud-colored vest, striped trousers, spats, straw hat and flowing tie, carrying a black doctor's bag.*)

NURSE: Right in here, Doctor.

DR.: Thank you, Miss Parker. (NURSE *exits, leaving door slightly ajar.*) Good afternoon, gentlemen. I'm Dr. Berserk. (*The boys watch as the doctor places black bag on table, taking out stethoscope, mallet, large hypodermic syringe, and needle. Starts adjusting needle.*) Now, which is the patient?

127

OLLIE: (*Indicating* STAN.) He is.

STAN: I'm not the patient. (*Points to* OLLIE.) *He's* the one who's insanitary.

OLLIE: (*To* STAN.) How dare you make such a statement? Why, I've never seen you before in my life. I don't know you from Adam.

STAN: Adam who?

DR.: Now, just a minute. (*To* OLLIE.) Who are you?

OLLIE: My name, sir, is Mr. Ticklebottom.

DR.: Then what are you doing here?

OLLIE: I came to visit a relative and got in this room by mistake.

STAN: Ohhh!

DR.: (*Turns quickly to* STAN.) Do you know this gentleman?

STAN: Do I know him? He's my father!

DR.: Father? Impossible. Why there's as much difference between you two as an elephant and a flea.

OLLIE: You see, Doctor, he's nuts. Positively balmy.

DR.: I'll soon find out. I'll make a test. (*To* STAN.) You first.

STAN: Go ahead. There's nothing wrong with *my* geranium.

DR.: (*Takes pencil out of pocket.*) Now, put your left hand over the right eye. (STAN *puts his hand over* DOCTOR's *right eye.*) Not mine! (STAN *crosses over, puts his hand over* OLLIE's *eye.*) No, no—*your* eye! (*Business of* STAN *trying to cross arms, getting them tangled up.* DOCTOR *finally grabs* STAN's *hand and correctly places it over*

STAN's *eye. He waves pencil back and forth in front of* STAN's *eyes several times.* STAN *suddenly starts to faint; leans toward* OLLIE.)

OLLIE: What's the matter? (*Straightens* STAN *up.*)

STAN: I feel dizzy. (DOCTOR *continues to move pencil back and forth.*)

DR.: Now, what does that look like?

STAN: Do it again. (DOCTOR *repeats business.*)

DR.: What does it look like?

STAN: A monkey in a cage. (DOCTOR *does big take.*)

DR.: I believe you're nuttier than a fruit cake.

STAN: What are you trying to do, make a mountain out of my mole?

OLLIE: Well, now that you're convinced, Doctor, I guess I'll be going.

DR.: Just a minute. I'm not through yet. (*To* OLLIE.) Now you. Cross your legs, close your eyes, and touch the tip of your nose.

OLLIE: With my leg?

STAN: No, he means like this. (*Demonstrates as he talks.*) Cross your legs, close your eyes and touch the tip of your nose. (*As* STAN *says the last, he puts thumb to nose.*)

DR.: (*Bowing to* OLLIE.) You may go.

STAN: (*Opens eyes.*) Thank you, Doctor. (*Starts out,* DOCTOR *grabs him.*)

DR.: Not you. You should be in a straitjacket. (*Turning back to* OLLIE.) Well, goodbye, Mr. . . . er . . . ah . . .

OLLIE: Hardy.

DR.: Hardy?

OLLIE: Hardybottom. Well, goodbye, Doctor. (*Starts toward door.*)

STAN: Goodbye, Ollie.

OLLIE: Goodbye, Stanley.

DR.: (*Takes it big.*) Ollie . . . Stanley . . . just a minute. (*Suspiciously, to* OLLIE.) Are you sure you don't know him?

OLLIE: Of course not. You just admitted, Doctor—he's balmy. So his word means absolutely nothing. (*To* STAN.) Does it?

STAN: Nothing.

OLLIE: (*To* DOCTOR.) You see, he admits it himself.

DR.: Sorry I detained you, Mr. Twinklebottom. I hope you'll forgive me.

OLLIE: It's all right, sir. (*Shakes hands with* DOCTOR.) No hard feelings. (NURSE *enters, unseen by* OLLIE.) Merry Christmas— (*to* STAN) Snow White! (OLLIE *tries to shake* STAN's *hand.* STAN *slaps* OLLIE's *hand away, tries to hit him.*)

STAN: I'll get even with you for this. (DOCTOR *interferes, trying to stop* STAN.)

OLLIE: Take good care of him, Doctor. (*Starts out, bows to*

NURSE *as he passes.*) Goodbye. (*Does big take when he recognizes* NURSE.)

NURSE: Just where do you think you're going?

DR.: That's all right, Nurse. This is Mr. Bottom-something. He made a mistake and got in the wrong room.

OLLIE: Thank you, Doctor. (*To* NURSE *as he starts to exit.*) Pardon me, madam.

NURSE: (*Pulls him back from door.*) Oh no, you don't. Get right back in bed. (*Pushes him.*) Come on, Cock Robin.

DR.: What's going on here? What's this all about?

NURSE: He tried to escape, and I caught him just in time.

DR.: You've made a mistake, Miss Parker. This is the patient, and this is the nurse. (*To* OLLIE.) Now, Mr. Bottomley, when did these bird-like symptoms appear first?

STAN: Just this morning, Doctor.

DR.: This morning? As recent as that?

STAN: Yes. He said he felt like flying around with the birds.

OLLIE: Don't pay any attention to him, Doctor. I can explain everything.

DR.: You can explain nothing. (*Turns back to* STAN.) You say he wanted to fly around with the birds?

STAN: (*Taking full advantage of the situation to get back at* OLLIE.) That's right—and he started flapping his arms— and jumped right out the window. You should have seen him go.

DR.: Incredible! (NURSE *suddenly discovers the two eggs* STAN *brought.*)

NURSE: Where did these eggs come from?

STAN: Oh, those. (*Pointing to* OLLIE.) He laid them! (NURSE *and* DOCTOR *take this big.*)

DR.: He laid them? (*Turns to* NURSE.) Good gracious, put those in a safe place where they won't get broken. I want them to be analyzed. (NURSE *looks around for a safe place to put them, opens nightstand door, and puts them inside.*)

DR.: (*To* STAN.) Now, after he laid the eggs, what happened? (STAN *looks toward bed, sees pillow and gets idea.*)

STAN: He tried to molt!

DR.: Started to molt? Are you sure? (STAN *crosses to bed.*)

STAN: Am I sure? (*Takes handful of feathers, throws them in the air.*)

DR.: Good heavens, this is really serious. (*To* NURSE.) Quick, Nurse. Make arrangements for an immediate operation. This is an emergency.

NURSE: Right away, Doctor. (NURSE *exits.* DOCTOR *takes a packet of bird seed from bag on table. Puts some in a little metal cup. As he pours*):

DR.: In the meantime, I'll make a final test. (*Hands cup to* OLLIE.) Here, swallow this.

OLLIE: What is it?

DR.: It's the famous Dr. Wombat's birdseed test.

OLLIE: (*Refusing to take cup.*) I'm no bird. What are you trying to do, poison me?

DR.: Nonsense, it can't do you any harm. (*Hands cup to* STAN.) Here, hold this. (*Crosses to* OLLIE.)

OLLIE: What are you going to do?

DR.: Now, take it easy. I'm not going to hurt you. This is for your own good. (DOCTOR *takes* OLLIE *by nose and chin, opens mouth wide. Turns to* STAN.) Now, you. Pour it down the throat.

STAN: What?

DR.: Pour it down the throat! (STAN, *not thinking, pours it down his own throat.* DOCTOR *watches, appalled.*) Not you! (DOCTOR *takes cup away from* STAN *and refills it.* STAN *crosses over to* OLLIE.)

STAN: Try some. It's swell! (DOCTOR *hands refilled cup to* OLLIE.)

DR.: Come on now, drink it down.

OLLIE: What's it for?

DR.: This will make you sing. Then we can tell what kind of bird you think you are—a canary or a buzzard.

OLLIE: Oh, well, then. I've got nothing to worry about. (OLLIE *pours it down, swallowing with difficulty.* NURSE *enters.*)

NURSE: Everything is prepared, doctor.

DR.: Good, we'll operate in ten minutes. (*To* OLLIE.) Now you just relax while I get ready. (*To* NURSE.) Be sure he doesn't get out, Miss Parker.

(DOCTOR *and* NURSE *exit.* STAN *and* OLLIE *sit for a minute.* STAN *gets up, starts gathering his belongings, puts sandwich in paper bag with the flowers. Starts toward door, turns to tell* OLLIE *goodbye, but instead starts to chirp like a bird.* OLLIE *tries to answer, and he starts chirping. Then they hold ad-lib chirping conversation until point where* DOCTOR *and* NURSE *enter. Both react big.*)

DR.: (*To* NURSE.) Quick, get those eggs and rush them to the dissection room! (NURSE *opens cabinet, lets out a scream as two pigeons fly out, leaving some eggshells. All take it big. Very loud chirping sounds. Pandemonium reigns.*)

BLACKOUT

Four

It was a blessing of great dimension, easily the prime blessing of his personal life, that Stan met Ida Kitaeva Raphael. Ida, at the time of their first meeting, was not long a widow. Her late husband, billed simply in the world's concert halls as Raphael, was probably the best concertinist who ever lived and had had an extraordinarily distinguished career. Ida was born in China of White Russian parents, and was on the concert stage when she married Raphael and began traveling with him. After her husband's death, she decided to settle in Hollywood in the hope that she might obtain work in films as a singer. She says of her first meeting with Stan:

Ida:

"I was working with Preston Sturges, a dear friend, on his Harold Lloyd film, *The Sin of Harold Diddlebock.* This was in early 1945. I had worked for Preston also in his *Hail the Conquering Hero.* I played a foreign prima donna in that. He liked me so much in *Hail* that after seeing the rushes, he said, 'Madame Raphael, I wish I had known you sang so well, I would have used you earlier, throughout the picture.' I was so nervous doing that work I could cry, but we became wonderful friends. He was like a father to me. Anyway, one day after the *Hail* film, I got a call from Preston about the Harold Lloyd film. I came to the studio; it was very informal, a drink while we talked in the late afternoon.

"Anyway, there was a gentleman sitting there next to us and Preston introduced him to me. I didn't pay much attention to his name. Then the gentleman said goodbye and left. Then Preston said to me, 'Madame, I want you to be in the new Harold Lloyd picture. Mr. Lloyd, of course, was the gentleman who just left.' I almost fell over. Mr. Lloyd wasn't wearing his glasses and I didn't recognize him. Everyone around us was hysterical: they thought it was so funny.

"So I started to work on the *Diddlebock* picture, and it took a long time. But I was well paid and always on salary even though Mr. Sturges took his time making it—and there were also release problems, I believe. Anyway this was now early in 1945. My quitting time on the set was about 6 P.M. A girl friend of mine had a Russian restaurant in the Valley —the Moskwa—and she had been after me for a long time to come to the restaurant. So, one night, I had the strangest feeling—an instinct, you would call it—to go visit my friend's restaurant.

"I didn't have transportation, no car, didn't even know how to drive—so a gentleman from the studio dropped me off at the restaurant on his way home. At the Moskwa I had a marvelous dinner and a pleasant time with my friend. While I was having dinner, the door opened and in walked a party of about ten people, very noisy, happy, lots of laughter. My friend, the owner of the restaurant, and I were sitting at the far end of the room. The party that walked in went to their reserved table in the center of the restaurant, and my friend rose to greet them in a very friendly way, especially this one gentleman at the head of the table. She then came back to sit with me and said, 'You know who that is?' 'I haven't the slightest idea,' I said. She said, 'That's Stan Laurel!' 'Who's Stan Laurel?' I asked her. 'Why, he's a big movie star,' she said. I hadn't seen any of his movies—I didn't go to movies much—so I didn't know who he was. I paid no attention to him. It just didn't have any meaning to me—who Stan Laurel was.

"Anyway, some minutes later—and I was young then, looking good, very well dressed, this evening particulariy— my friend had been talking again to the party of people, and she came back and said, 'He wants to talk to you, this Stan Laurel.' So I said, '*Me?* O.K.,' and I laughed. He came over and she introduced him. And he was very nice, and we talked, talked, talked, and pretty soon it looked as if he didn't want to go back to his party. But I still didn't think about all this too much. It was nice but that was all. Later, I found out a girl in that party was dying to get him. So he finally went back to join them. When the party left, Stan came over, very gracious, said goodbye to me, said he'd like to meet me again. I didn't think anything of it.

"A few days passed and my restaurant friend called me and said, 'Stan Laurel keeps calling, he really wants to meet you.' She kept after me and kept after me until I came down to the Moskwa again to have dinner with Stan. We met again several times for dinner, and I still didn't realize he was such a big star. I thought maybe I should go see one of his pictures to see what he did in the movies. So we began to date for some months, and I began to realize what a wonderful man he was, so wonderful inside, such a good man. I didn't know yet he was a genius. Then one night he said to me, 'I want to propose to you but I'm not divorced yet. Here we go—that word *again!*' So we met and agreed the very next day, and he sent me a big box of roses—twenty-four. It was so exciting. He explained to me he was between pictures and I could tell he had been unhappy with the studio. I was still working with Preston Sturges, and Stan offered to drive me to the studio every day. I felt so very bad —poor darling, here he was the big star, and not working. He lived then in his beautiful home, Fort Laurel, in Canoga Park.

"Then came May 1946, and he was in process of divorce. Ben Shipman called Stan one day—I was visiting him at Canoga Park—and told him the divorce finally came through. So the next day we drove to Yuma, Arizona, to get married, and we drove all afternoon, drove and drove. Finally, I smell some country smells—cows and barns and all that—and I said, 'Wait a moment. Where are we going? I think you've lost your way because I think we've wound up on the range.'

"He *had* lost his way. It kept getting dark, then darker, and we got to Yuma very late because of this being lost. And the judge had to get up out of bed to marry us, just like a Laurel and Hardy movie. Then we got in the car and drove all night to San Diego where we put up in the Grand Hotel. In the meantime, there were headlines in the Los Angeles newspapers, WHERE IS STAN LAUREL? They had sent reporters to all the railroad stations and the like.

"Well, the reporters found us, and Stan told them to come up. So they came into our rooms, taking pictures, asking questions. I was so nervous. But they were nice. There was one kind newspaperman there who gave me a picture of Stan and me taken right there as a present to us. I love that picture, it's really our wedding picture. So—here the newspapermen were all piled into the room and asking questions. So I said to them all, 'Please! Please, you boys quote me. Be sure it's accurate: *no more divorces for Stan Laurel!*' They laughed. My God!

"But I was right. There weren't any more. And we had twenty wonderful, happy years.

"People ask me what kind of person Stan really was. Well, I knew him better than anyone, and the only word I can use about him to describe him really is 'wonderful.' Of course he had the greatest sense of humor of any human being I ever met or ever will meet. My God, how we laughed! And such a generous man! He supported lots of people, even when he was between jobs himself. He loved my family, and it pleased me so much one day when I overheard him telling my brother, Mark, when they were sitting in our kitchen, that he, Stan, was so thrilled to play vaudeville in England now that he had a marvelous girl. I was very happy to hear that.

"When he wasn't working, there were still so many expenses, especially the alimony. In fact, money wasn't so good with him when we were talking about marriage. He said,

'You know, I can't even afford a proper ring, the kind of ring you should have, a wedding ring.' I said, 'But we can use my first wedding ring,' and he said, 'Well, if you don't mind.' There were so many money demands on him that he couldn't afford even an engagement ring. So the engagement ring came later when he was making good money in England. Then things were all right again financially.

"Stan's heart was so big. He kept actors, acrobats, lots of people who were broke, out at the Canoga Park ranch. Even when he had little, he gave them money. He even helped some comedians from the Roach studios (whose names I won't mention) when they were broke (and which they never paid back). He was a marvelous man, Stan. Of course he was temperamental like all artists, and he could be quick-tempered. I used to kid him about his quick temper, and say it was because of his red hair. When he was a boy, he was called 'Ginger.'

"He was very unhappy when he wasn't working. You can imagine, not being able to do the thing he loved and did so well. Then when Delfont offered him the chance to play the music halls, he got so excited and happy. We went over in 1947 on the *Queen Mary,* first class, and I was seasick all the way. But Stan loved every minute of it. Wouldn't miss a single meal. When we got to London, the Waterloo Station, it was raining terribly, and there were thousands of people waiting to see Stan and Babe. That upset Stan because he hated people to be inconvenienced, waiting like that in the downpour. Stan and Babe rehearsed in London with Harry Marigny who played the license examiner, and then we went up to northern England, to Newcastle, which was practically Stan's home town.

"Stan was so very thrilled to be playing in English music halls again. But the theatre at Newcastle had no heat, it was freezing backstage. That night the boys were a smash. Mr. Delfont was ecstatic and the boys were so happy because they had such a great success. We went back to the Newcastle railway station hotel where we were staying, the three of us. Lucille [Hardy] was still in California, recuperating from a little operation. When we got back to the hotel, it was just like the theatre—freezing. It was deathly cold in our room, and Babe sat with us to talk as we went over the great success they'd had.

"Then Babe called Lucille in California to see how she was feeling. She told him it was ninety degrees in California and that made us feel very miserable. There was only one tiny, tiny fireplace in that big hotel room. Coal was still being rationed then, and we had just a few pieces. I laid down on the bed in my coat and galoshes trying to get warm. But Babe didn't mind so much. He was always warm and perspiring, and that night he was wearing a California robe. Stan and I were the cold ones. So then Stan put the last piece of coal on the fire, looked down at it and said very solemnly, 'There'll always be an England!'

"Oh, how we laughed at that! We just all broke up, burst into such laughter. It was so funny at the time. We got hysterical. Babe was roaring with laughter, his stomach going up and down so. Oh, my darling Stan, such a sense of humor.

"One time we were playing in a theatre there—at Bolton,

a really dirty, drafty old theatre. Stan wanted to send out for some fish and chips. Stan adored fish and chips.

"But the stage doorman protested—he said indignantly fish and chips would smell up the place. Stan just looked at the man, and took a deep breath, getting that backstage air in his lungs. 'Bring the fish and chips, please,' he told the man politely. 'They'll be like perfume to the air floating around in here now.'

"Stan and Babe had such a great success all over England. Full houses, audiences just dying to see Laurel and Hardy. Then we went to France where the boys played at the Lido in Paris. The Lido cabaret. It was a bad place to do *The Drivers' License Sketch,* because it was a night club, big, noisy, and with drunks around. And Stan always wanted perfect conditions when he did anything. Also, the sketch was in English, of course, and few people understood it. And then on top of that, backstage the chorus girls were running around absolutely naked, and Stan protested to the manager because parents and kids came back to visit Stan and Babe, and Stan didn't want them to see the nudity.

"The French have always loved Laurel and Hardy very, very much, and when we went over in 1950 to make *Atoll K,* President Vincent Auriol of France gave a special luncheon for Stan and Babe—no women allowed—so there was no translator for Stan. Imagine! He sat next to the President of France and could only communicate in pantomime. I wish I could have seen that."

After the overwhelmingly successful 1947 tour and the 1950–51 trauma of *Atoll K,* Stan's affections were even more strongly engaged to British vaudeville. He began his career in music halls and he was willing to end it there, coming over to England seasonally as long as health and public demand continued strong. In 1952 as they made their second vaudeville tour, he had little reason to think the vigor of either would alter. Stan loved the English music hall. It had nurtured him, and from it he drew a number of his standard comic devices: the bowler hat, the deep comic gravity, and above all, the gentle nonsensical understatement. His boyhood hero was Dan Leno (1860–1904), the greatest of British music hall comedians. Stan, despite knowing the greatest music hall acts firsthand, never saw Leno in person, but he collected Leno recordings and he knew many performers who either directly or indirectly imitated Leno. Leno has been described as "the epitome of Cockney comedy, of domestic humor, and resignation." One of Leno's stocks-in-trade was the long, rambling nonsensical anecdote, a device which Stan took up and made his own in abbreviated form. Frequently in the films Laurel would offer Hardy what seemed to be a fairly sensible suggestion. "Let me have that again, Stanley," the slightly puzzled Hardy would order. "Well—" became the Laurel prelude to a pointless, disconnected mangling of his previous suggestion.

In returning to the English music hall, Stan was coming home in a number of ways. In 1953, as we sat backstage at the Birmingham Hippodrome, he told me how glorious it felt to be back.

Stan:

"It's not the same as when I was a kid, of course. I miss the mateyness of the old days when there were so many more halls and so many more people in the profession. But even at that, it's a great thrill to go out there and hear that roar of laughter when you do a good one. *Birds of a Feather*, now, is broader than we'd do in the films, of course, but it's still the basic kind of nonsense Babe and I love. What we're doing now is really rather old-fashioned music hall. What I'd like to do one day is to appear in English pantomime, maybe even some films in that style."

Which is what he almost did.

Happily married at last, to Ida Kitaeva Raphael.

Copenhagen, 1947: Visiting the Carlsberg brewery with their wives...

Admiring their likenesses at a personal appearance...

...sampling the product, in a rare unguarded moment.

...and reflecting on two decades of harmonious partnership.

Clowning with Sir Harry Lauder at his home near Glasgow, 1947.

Stan and fans greet Babe on arrival at Gare St. Lazare, Paris, 1950.

Stan and Ida in their apartment at the Oceana Hotel, Santa
Monica, 1962.

At his desk, after a session of answering fan mail.

With director Tay Garnett (left), who wrote some of his early solo comedies, and Harry Lachman, who directed the team in "Our Relations." Circa 1963.

Five

After his death in 1965, at his widow's request, I went through Stan's papers and therein discovered his final legacy to the world of laughter. Written for the most part in his meticulous hand but also occasionally typewritten, on odd-sized bits of paper and stationery (including two paper napkins!), I found over a hundred Laurel and Hardy gags. Many of these contain ideas so rudimentary that he had not yet worked them out (Handkerchief gag. Three rubber bands stretched across the stage."); the meaning of others is also lost to us because of their even denser obscurity ("You're just my cup of tea."). But a number of the gags are splendidly clear.

In looking at these gags, it seemed to me that they were all discontinuous, just random bits and pieces which came to him at odd (sic) moments, impulsively jotted down for possible future use. But as I examined them and shuffled them about a bit, I began to see—after referring to notes I had taken in a 1963 conversation I had with Stan—that some of the gags were parts of an aborted television series Laurel and Hardy were contracted to do in 1954.

Also, I discovered, a few of the gags were created for Laurel and Hardy's personal appearances but had never been used. One such gag:

OLLIE: Thank you, ladies and gentlemen. It's sure nice to see you all again. You know, you haven't changed a bit. Have they, Stanley?

STAN: Not a bit—but they sure have altered.

OLLIE: What do you mean—altered?

STAN: Well, they're not sitting in the same places.

OLLIE: Do you mean to tell me you remember where everybody sat the last time we were here?

STAN: Certainly. (*Pointing to a guy in the audience.*) See Bill? He sat over there. (*Pointing to another seat.*)

OLLIE: Don't tell me you know them all by name?

STAN: Sure. (*To the guy in the audience.*) How are you, Bill?

GUY: I'm fine, Stan. (OLLIE *does a hell of a take.*)

The Hardy "take," of course, was a gigantic backward start of amazement, complete with wildly flailing arms.

Most of the gags and plot concepts left by Stan fall into the category of miscellany. Stan had little trouble working almost any kind of gag into the framework of films he was making, but some of the material he left was specifically crafted for the television films Laurel and Hardy were to make in 1954. Hal Roach, Jr., then in command of his father's studio, had signed his dad's old stars to do a series of hour-long television films in color. Stan was tremendously excited about these because once again he was to have total artistic control of their efforts and, in bountiful addition, he was returning to his boyhood. In conceiving the new films he was drawn irresistibly to the format of English pantomimes—the lively childlike "pantos" he had loved so much as a youth. These traditional Christmas entertainments of Great Britain are essentially fairy tales with much interwoven music, song, variety acts, and above all comic relief sometimes so extensive that *it* demands relief.

Laurel and Hardy were contracted to do four of these films, and if successful, there was little doubt that others would follow. For the series' title, Stan debated the choice of two names he conceived: The Fables of Laurel and Hardy, or Laurel and Hardy's Fabulous Fables. He rather inclined toward the latter. He had tentatively decided on eleven stories, the first four of which he began to structure in 1954:

> *Babes in the Woods*
>
> *Cinderella*
>
> *Little Red Riding Hood*
>
> *Jack and the Beanstalk*
>
> *Dick Whittington*
>
> *Beauty and the Beast*
>
> *Hop-o'-my-Thumb*
>
> *Aladdin*
>
> *Puss-in-Boots*
>
> *The Three Bears*
>
> *The Three Wishes*

Of these stories, he wrote but one, and that only in brief scenario. However, his outline gives an idea of the essential flavor of all the contemplated films. For *Babes in the Woods*, Stan conceived of Stanley and Ollie as comic villains much in the style of Stanlio and Ollio in one of their best films, *The Devil's Brother*. Stan's outline for *Babes in the Woods* reads:

"Two orphans (boy and girl) under guardianship of uncle. When of age, the kids inherit a fortune, including the castle, the village and all the countryside. The uncle schemes against them. Should they die, he will acquire the whole estate. Under a threat he engages two peace-loving vagabonds to do away with the children. They don't want to become involved but, their own lives at stake, they unwillingly accept. They try to kidnap the kids at night in their bedroom, but fail. They try again at a carnival in the village and this time succeed, by stealing a talking horse who rides the kids away to the woods where the vagabonds have decided to do the dirty work.

"They are followed by the kids' pet goat, much to the annoyance of the two vagabonds. On the way to the woods, it is discovered that the horse has lost one of its shoes—so they stop off at a blacksmith's shop to get a new one. The kids and horse have been missed in the village and a search for them is on. The horseshoe is found which gives a clue to the direction the kids were going.

"The vagabonds arrive in the woods but one of them (Stan) decides he won't have anything to do with it and ends up in a fight with the other (Ollie, who agrees with him but can't conceive of a way out of the dilemma). The goat helps Stan. The search party arrives and the vagabonds are arrested

—charged with intent to kill. They are about to be hanged but the talking horse gives evidence in their favor and accuses the uncle, who gets life imprisonment. And all live happily ever after. The vagabonds are forgiven by all and a Ball is given at the palace to celebrate the occasion."

This excursion into the world of childhood (with, however, gags amply provided for adult viewers) was an inevitable progression for Laurel and Hardy, two instinctive babes in the woods. "We made our pictures principally for adults, of course," Stan said to me, "but they were always loved by kids, too. I really hadn't realized how much kids watched us and loved us until the television reruns started. So I thought that in the new TV series we would maybe slant the pictures a little more toward the kids without in any way altering the way we created our regular gags."

For *Babes in the Woods*, he explained to me that they were going to lessen considerably the pratfalls and physical indignities they (and particularly Hardy) suffered in their films. "After all, we aren't thirty any more," he explained. Instead, quite in keeping with the fairy tale atmosphere of the new films, Stan wanted to go more deeply into the white magic which had characterized some of the business in their best films. One remembers from *Block-Heads* the pipe Stan formed by making a fist, stuffing it with tobacco, igniting it and puffing away quite satisfactorily on the thumb. In the same film, feeling the pangs of thirst, Stan casually pulls a full tumbler of water out of his coat pocket, and when the astounded Ollie sarcastically asks him why he doesn't put some *ice* in it, Stan reaches solemnly into his other pocket and produces several cubes. In *Way Out West* there is some hilarious byplay in which Stan, needing a match, uses his right thumb as he would a cigarette lighter. He casually flicks the thumb out from his curled fist and it flames up—again to the incredulous discomfort of Ollie.

The Fabulous Fables were to have a continuing series of white magic gags. One of the best has the boys on a journey during which Stan is ordered by Ollie to keep a record of meteorological changes.

OLLIE: Stanley, check which way the wind is blowing, please. (STAN *does so by throwing a stick in the air. When it comes down, he looks at it on the ground, marks "Down" on his chart. Later*):

OLLIE: Did you check on that wind again?

STAN: (*Nods.*) Down.

OLLIE: Down? There must be something wrong. Check it again. (STAN *throws the stick up in the air,* OLLIE *not watching. This time the stick doesn't come down. Later*):

OLLIE: Did you check on that wind again?

STAN (*Nods.*) Yes.

OLLIE: What was the result?

STAN: Up!

OLLIE: That's better. You see, it's always best to double-check. (OLLIE *walks along for a minute, then stops and looks very puzzled into the camera.*)

Stan had also contemplated similar gags in which the immutable forces of nature were mutated ("Bell falls off wall, hits Ollie on head. Stan goes to pick it up—it jumps away and rings loudly.") for insertion in the films. However, the principal comic texture of the Fabulous Fables was to be the benign and enchanting stupidity of Stan and Ollie—as ever were.

A gag typical of their endearing denseness is one in which the boys have tied up all their fortune in the sum of three one-dollar bills and a fifty-cent piece, with Stan for some incredible reason serving as keeper of the purse. In the course of their journey, Stan predictably loses the dollar bills. At some moment of great financial need, Ollie demands the money:

OLLIE: All right, give me the money. (STAN *hands over the fifty-cent piece.*) No, no! The folding money, the *folding* money! (*Hands back the fifty-cent piece to* STAN. STAN *eye-blinks, thinks profoundly, scratches his head. Then, brightly, he folds the coin in half and hands it back to* OLLIE.)

Ollie, of course, glares haplessly into the camera with his look of "What have I done to deserve this?" The pattern of Stan saying or doing something incredible, followed by Ollie's take, double-take or heart-rending camera look is a durable Laurel and Hardy hallmark. Sometimes the Laurel remark provoking the Hardy reaction has a kind of battered logic which causes Ollie to react in deferential puzzlement, as in this projected gag:

OLLIE: [*To a reluctant host.*] We'll only stay a few minutes.

STAN: Yes, we have to get along soon. We don't want to interfere with your dinner, do we, Ollie?

OLLIE: I should say not, Stanley. Not even if we were starving to death.

STAN: You know what, Ollie? That reminds me—we haven't eaten for three days: yesterday, today, and tomorrow. (*Ollie ponders that one.*)*

In the Fabulous Fables, they were always to be itinerants, moving quickly in and out of the various fairy tale adventures, complicating them in typical fashion. Many of their mishaps were to take place on the road as they went from event to event. One typical Laurel and Hardy mishap has them stop to rest by a roadside stream. Sending Stan to look at the milestone at road's edge, Ollie washes his stockings in the stream and as he dreamily trails them back and forth in the water, a vicious fish enters one of them, and Ollie puts the stocking back on. In his note on this, Stan does not spell out the complications resulting therefrom, specifying only "Babe reacts a hell of a lot." Stan returns from his charge to read the milestone—with the milestone in his arms. He can't read it, he says. Closeup of the milestone with an arrow and a legend, 20 MILES TO LONDON.

"Why, stupid," says Ollie, "that says 'Twenty miles to Lond—' Wait, just a moment, just a moment. Which way was the arrow pointing?" Stan, of course, cannot remember and goes into his classic tears when Ollie reacts with indignation. Stan's inability to read even the simplest words has long been a Laurel and Hardy staple, and in one of the Fables Stan had

* Stan had used this gag, simplified, in *One Good Turn* (1931).

planned their presence at an inn where they were to order dinner:

(STAN *picks up the menu, looks at it closely. Borrows* OLLIE's *spectacles, looks at the menu again. Shakes his head and hands them back.*)

OLLIE: Can't you see through them?
STAN: Oh, yes!
OLLIE: Then what's the matter?
STAN: I can't read.
OLLIE: Why did you borrow them then?
STAN: You *said* they were *reading* glasses!

And it is at this point that Stan's specific gags for the Fabulous Fables end. That he had others in mind was certain because he had told me of a sequence he was developing in his mind about Stan and Ollie thinking each other the source of impertinent remarks which actually came from the talking horse in *Babes in the Woods*. However, Stan never confided this to paper. What now follows are gags and ideas of a general nature, some of which he intended to work into the Fables, others of which he hoped one day to use for a film of contemporary life. He had only the most nebulous idea of the latter project, but envisioned it pretty much the mixture as before—Laurel and Hardy up against the moils of an increasingly complex world. In any case, Stan rarely prepared detailed outlines of his films before shooting. He usually had a very general idea of story, together with some typical gags, which he would bring into a conference with the Roach writers and gag men. From these sessions would come a more or less formal script which would serve as the outline for their work but it was outline only. Frequently on the day of shooting Stan would alter the material and/or lines if something funnier came to him, as it frequently did. It was understood on the Roach lot that this was the standard operating procedure, a procedure sturdily ignored at 20th Century-Fox.

Herewith, then, presented in their miscellaneous form, are the additional gags and ideas which Stan had hoped to use in future films. Some, obviously, are not as funny as others but most of them, it is important to remember, were certain to suffer a happy sea change by being refined into more memorably comic form by Stan at the time of shooting.

* * *

Ollie is reading aloud a description of the subject on the base of a statue, and the text includes the word "myth."

STAN: Myth?

OLLIE: Certainly. (*Scornfully.*) Do you mean to tell me you don't know what a *myth* is?

STAN: (*Proudly.*) I certainly do.

OLLIE: All right, then, just what is it?

STAN: A myth is a moth's *sister!*

* * *

Stan in writing out the word "summer," spells it aloud as he scrawls it painfully, and slowly.

STAN: S, u, m, b, e, r.

OLLIE: That's not how you spell "summer." You spell it, s, u, m, *m*, e, r.

154

STAN: Then how come you spell "plumber," p, l, u, m, *b*, e, r? (OLLIE *is totally baffled.*)

* * *

Stan, in explaining something to Ollie, looks around to see if anyone is listening, then turns back to his pal, only to find Ollie looking apprehensively the other way. In consequence, Stan looks fearfully in the direction Ollie has been looking. Ollie thinking Stan has *really* seen something fearful, looks with horror at what he believes Stan has seen. Stan by now has turned around and is looking the other way in ascending fear, and Ollie follows through the same pattern of increasing apprehensions until:

OLLIE: Just a moment. What are you *looking* at?

STAN: I was looking at what you were looking at.

OLLIE: But I was looking at what *you* were looking at.

STAN: Well, what was I looking at?

OLLIE: That's what I want to know. What *were* you looking at?

STAN: (*Eye-blinks, head scratches.*) Do you like fried duck?

* * *

A Stanley aphorism delivered to a bewildered Ollie: "Never kiss a dog until you look up his pedigree."

* * *

Stan and Ollie are in the post office.

OLLIE: I beg your pardon, sir, but we'd like to see the General.

CLERK: The General? What General?

STAN: General Delivery. He has two letters for us.

* * *

STAN: I don't like noiseless typewriters.

OLLIE: Why on earth not?

STAN: Well, you can't hear when you make a mistake.

* * *

Stan and Ollie at the ticket window of a train station.

OLLIE: Two return tickets, please.

CLERK: Where to?

OLLIE: Why, back *here*, of course.

* * *

Stan comes home with a package. He tells Ollie it's a beautiful smoking jacket which he just got as a bargain at a fire sale. He takes the jacket from the package, holds it up admiringly —and smoke comes out of the pockets.

* * *

OLLIE: What's that on your shoe?

STAN: A corn pad.

OLLIE: Why've you got it on the *outside* of your shoe?

STAN: If I put it inside, I can't get my shoe on.

* * *

Montage. A tracking shot of Stan and Ollie's feet as they walk along a sidewalk. To indicate passage of time, every second sidewalk square is labeled with the name of a month. After four or five months have been walked over, Stan's feet jump over the next one.

OLLIE: What's that for?

STAN: Leap year!

* * *

A shot of Stan playing the piano, keyboard not visible. He rolls through several astounding, intricate arpeggios worthy of Artur Rubinstein. Ollie looks on, dumbfounded. When Stan reaches up to turn over the sheet of music, we see he is wearing boxing gloves. Ollie looks at the camera, lifting his arms in helplessness.

* * *

Another Stanley aphorism to the befuddled Ollie: "Remember—if you save nothing, you can't take it with you."

* * *

Stan always hoped he might somehow be able to work in a gag in which he was required to wear a camel's-hair coat. The coat would be the conventional camel's-hair coat—with a hump on the back.

* * *

STAN: I can't read with these glasses.

OLLIE: Here, use this. (*Hands* STAN *an eyeglass cleansing tissue.*) One of these will fix you up.

STAN: (*Takes off his glasses, rubs the tissue on his eyes. Picks up book and starts to read.*) Say, you're right.

* * *

Scene: OLLIE's office. He is busy at his desk, sticking blue chip stamps into a book. Knock at the door.

OLLIE: Come in! (STAN *enters.*) You don't have to knock every time. That's only when I'm in conference with myself. It's most disturbing. Everytime I'm doing something important, all I hear is knock, knock, knock.

STAN: Knock, knock?

OLLIE: (*Not thinking.*) Who's there?

STAN: Sandy.

OLLIE: Sandy who?

STAN: San Diego.

OLLIE: Stop bothering me!

STAN: But this is important.

OLLIE: All right, what is it?

STAN: A man outside wants to talk to you.

OLLIE: Who is it?

STAN: He says he's the invisible man.

OLLIE: Stop wasting my time!

STAN: All right—I'll tell him you can't see him.

OLLIE: Who did you say it was?

STAN: The invisible man.

OLLIE: What does he look like?

STAN: Well, he . . . uh—you'd better see for yourself.

* * *

STAN: I'm so hungry, I'm starving to death.

OLLIE: Why don't you eat something?

STAN: I don't want to spoil my appetite.

* * *

Stan, after tentative tasting of a Christmas plum pudding he has made, says, "It's good—but it sure tastes lousy." He then suggests they ignite it for proper Christmas effect, and pours a half bottle of liquor over it. Ollie lights it and it flames up wildly, putting the entire room on fire. After the holocaust is hosed out, Ollie looks at the pudding on the plate, now burned down to the size and texture of a charred pea. He eats it as he says *"Merry* Christmas" to Stan. "By the way, Stanley, where did you get that liquor?" Stan holds up a bottle, and Ollie goes into a spasm as he reads the label, "Paint remover."

* * *

Ollie with a hangover: "My head is as clear as a bell. It keeps ringing all the time."

* * *

STAN: My—you look like a million dollars.

OLLIE: (*Scornfully.*) You never *saw* a million dollars.

STAN: That's right. You look like nothing I ever saw.

* * *

Stan has difficulty in dialing a telephone number: his finger keeps slipping out of the hole. Finally he pulls a billiard chalk out of his pocket, chalks the end of his finger and satisfactorily completes the call.

* * *

The next morning after their house burns down, Ollie stands before the wreckage.

OLLIE: I wonder how the fire started?

STAN: I don't know. It was burning when I went to sleep.

* * *

Story fragment. "Ollie falls in love and is too bashful to woo and propose to the girl. He asks Stan to be his emissary but

Stan declines. Ollie bribes him; Stan accepts. Ollie says, 'Ask her if she'll marry me.' Stan says to the girl, 'Ollie wants to know if you'll marry me.' He gives her flowers and an engagement ring which she accepts as coming from Stan. (Bring Father and family into it.) Ollie is watching through window of home, horrified. Decides to break up the romance. Knocks on door, Father opens door, Ollie accidentally hits Father with clenched fist, knocking him out. Ollie denounces Stan but Father, sore at being knocked out, refuses to listen to Ollie. Stan, fearing Ollie, wants to back out of marriage but Father threatens breach of promise suit if he does. (Father owns blacksmith shop and is also justice of peace.) Ollie tries to stop the affair, paints spots on Stan's face while he is asleep, wakes him up—smallpox!"

* * *

The boys are playing poker. Each keeps raising. Finally:

OLLIE: What have you got?

STAN: A queen!

OLLIE: (*Throws down his cards.*) And I thought you were bluffing!

* * *

A scene with Laurel and Hardy and a third character. Ollie is explaining confidentially to the third person, "Between you, me and the gate post—" Stan thinks he is being referred to as the gate post and cries.

* * *

Stan saws on the small end of a board. The entire opposite, very lengthy, part falls off.

*   *   *

Stan thought it was almost worth the effort to do a Pilgrims-Thanksgiving Day picture just to do this sequence. He conceived of a running gag to kid the vast number of people who claim descent from the Pilgrims. The gag would show the *Mayflower* disgorging endless processions of passengers —thousands upon thousands leaving the tiny boat in cut back shots all through the picture.

*   *   *

The following is approximately half the dialogue Stan wrote for a two-reeler he planned to make in the mid-1930s. By that time, of course, Laurel and Hardy had already made feature films but Stan persisted in his affection for the shorter film. It was during the writing of this dialogue, following a conversation with Roach, that Stan realized the two-reel film form was probably gone forever. He kept this dialogue sequence, however, and appended a one-word note to it, "Maybe?" Part of it indeed was used for their 1935 short, *Thicker Than Water*. Stan, Ollie, and Ollie's wife have just finished dinner. Stan is cleaning up his plate happily, licking his spoon, his plate, etc.

STAN: (*To* MRS. HARDY.) Gee, that was good. I'm full up. Funny, I don't feel a bit hungry now.

WIFE: (*Sarcastically.*) I'm full up, too.

STAN: You are? Well, if you can't eat your pie, I'll finish it up for you. Waste not, want not. (*Takes her pie.*)

WIFE: Put that down. (*Takes plate from him.*)

STAN: Sorry. I thought you were full up.

WIFE: I am full up—and *fed* up.

OLLIE: What's the matter, honey?

WIFE: What's the matter? You brought this tapeworm friend of yours to live with us as a boarder, six months ago. He's eating me out of house and home, and hasn't paid me a cent for his room and board yet.

STAN: I certainly have!

WIFE: You certainly haven't!

STAN: I certainly have. (*To* OLLIE.) Haven't I?

WIFE: What's he got to do with it?

STAN: I gave it to him.

WIFE: What for?

STAN: He said he was the boss here. (OLLIE *spits out his coffee.* STAN *picks up wife's pie and starts to eat it.*)

WIFE: (*Grabs pie.*) You leave that alone. (*To* OLLIE.) So you're the boss, eh? (*Breaks plate on his head.*) Where's that money?

OLLIE: (*Hands over cash.*) I thought I'd save it for you, honey. (*Coyly.*) And surprise you at Christmas!

WIFE: From now on, I'll surprise myself—once a week.

OLLIE: The lunch was lovely, darling. Well, come, Stanley. It's getting late.

WIFE: Where do you think *you're* going?

OLLIE: We're going to the races.

WIFE: Oh, no, you're not. If you think you're going to walk out and leave me with a lot of dirty dishes—you're mistaken.

STAN: (*To* OLLIE.) Well, I'll see you later.

OLLIE: Oh no, you don't. You're going to stay here and help me.

STAN: I don't have to stay here. (*To* WIFE.) Do I?

WIFE: You can do what you like and I wish you would. (*Exit.*)

STAN: Thank you, honey! (OLLIE *glares.*) I mean, Mrs. Hardy.

OLLIE: (*Pushes* STAN.) Help me with these dishes. The sooner we get them done the quicker.

STAN: The quicker what?

OLLIE: Never mind. Hurry up and let's get going.

STAN: O.K. (*Puts on hat and starts for door.*) I'll help you when we get back.

OLLIE: Say, that's a good idea. (*Calls wife.*) Molly-o! Oh, honey—yoo hoo. Molly-o! (WIFE *enters.*) Stan just thought of a splendid idea.

WIFE: This I've got to hear. Well, what is it, Einstein?

STAN: Well, *he* said, "Let's get going"—and I said "I'll help you with the dishes when we get back."

OLLIE: Isn't that a good idea, honey? We'll wash the dishes when we come back.

WIFE: (*Hits* OLLIE *with frying pan. He slides to the floor —out.*) You mean when you come *to!* (*Exit.*)

STAN: (*Business of reviving* OLLIE. *Then both start to wash dishes. Business to be arranged:* OLLIE *washing,* STAN *wiping,* STAN *putting washed dishes in pile that* OLLIE *starts to wash, keeps going until* OLLIE *notices minutes later that no dishes have been washed, and when dishes done, all dishes are broken anyway. Following dialogue during business of doing dishes:*)

STAN: I wonder if that horse will run today.

OLLIE: Which one?

STAN: Molly-o. It's a hundred to one.

OLLIE: Molly-o? That's my wife's name. Sounds like a good omen. Wish I knew. I'd put everything I've got on it.

STAN: I can find out maybe.

OLLIE: How?

STAN: I know a feller who lives next door to a guy who doesn't have to work.

OLLIE: Why?

STAN: He knows a relative of the jockey's grandfather—the same jockey that's riding Molly-o, and he gets his tips from him. Right on the nose!

OLLIE: You mean that guy wins so much he doesn't have to work?

STAN: Never done a day's work since he was three years old.

OLLIE: Where's this friend of yours that knows this guy?

STAN: I don't know. Haven't seen him for years. He used to hang around the Do 'Em Inn Pub.

OLLIE: Why don't you phone there and see if he's still around? If we get a tip on Molly-o—bang goes the whole works. Right on the nose.

STAN: (*Phones. Arrange dialogue. Gets party who will find out and call back.*) He'll call us back.

OLLIE: Good. Now let's see—how much can I scrape together?

STAN: How much have you got in the bank?

OLLIE: (*Confidentially.*) We've got nothing in the bank. (*Big take.*) Besides it's none of your business. Molly-o wouldn't like me to discuss our financial affairs with anyone.

STAN: Well, if you won't tell me—you figure it out yourself. How about pawning her jewelry?

OLLIE: They're already in— Stop prying into my private affairs! (*Phone rings.* STAN *in conversation, arrange dialogue.*)

STAN: He says it's all set. Put everything you can beg, borrow, and steal.

Here the manuscript ends. The only thing virtually predictable about the film's ending is that the repeated phrase "Right on the nose" is going to have some kind of visual pay-off, most likely with Hardy the recipient and his wife the donor.

Among his papers, I discovered part of another Laurel scenario. The date of composition is uncertain but it must be about 1931. A very small portion of the dialogue was used for the foreign release print of *Laughing Gravy*, a two-reeler made that year.

SCENE: *attic,* OLLIE *preparing scanty meal.* "No cooking" *sign on wall. Knock on door.* OLLIE *hurriedly puts things away and tries to blow away smoke, etc. Opens door. It is* STAN. OLLIE *is very annoyed.*)

OLLIE: Why didn't you *say* it was you?

STAN: I didn't want to disturb you. I thought you might be having a beauty sleep. (OLLIE *gives him a dirty look, starts to get dishes & cooking utensils out again and begins cooking.*) Say—maybe it would be a good idea if we had a signal so we would both know who it was.

OLLIE: (*Sarcastically.*) Splendid! What would you suggest?

STAN: Well, when I want to come in, I'll call "Yoo hoo!" Then you call "Hoo yoo!" Then *I'll* call "Mee hoo!" Then you open the door—and you'll know right away "Who's who!" Let's try it. (STAN *exits to hallway. Closes door, then knocks from outside.*) Yoo hoo! (LANDLORD *appears behind him.*)

OLLIE: Hoo yoo!

STAN: (*Sees* LANDLORD, *doesn't know what to do. Quickly*): *Him* hoo! (OLLIE *opens door,* LANDLORD *enters, followed by* STAN. OLLIE *takes it big, attempts to put cooking things away in a wild scramble. Stops, looks guilty, tie twiddles.*)

LANDLORD: (*Yelling.*) I told you no cooking in here, and I'm telling you I'm giving you until tomorrow to pay up three weeks' rent you owe me. (*Exits, slamming door, causing the little pan of stew to fall off stove into* OLLIE's *lap, things fall off walls, etc.*)

OLLIE: (*Looking disgusted at* STAN.) Yoo *hoo!* Well, here's another fine mess you've gotten me into. Did you find a job for us?

STAN: I found one, but I can't take it yet.

OLLIE: What do you mean, you didn't take it? We've *got* to work. We've got to pay our rent and eat. Who do you think you *are* to turn down the opportunity of me making a living? Tell *me* where the job is. I'll go right now and start to work right away. (*Puts on coat.*) You've got a lot of nerve interfering with my livelihood —standing in my way to fortune. Don't smile. Remember—"Tall Oaks from Little Acorns Grow."

STAN: I wasn't smiling. My face must have slipped.

OLLIE: Well, pick it up and come on. (*All ready to go.*)

STAN: (*Hesitating.*) I don't want to go—

OLLIE: Why?

STAN: Well—

OLLIE: Well what?

STAN: They only wanted *me*—said they didn't want any part of you.

OLLIE: (*Staggered.*) So they didn't want *me*, eh? I see it all now. You don't want me either. You make up this story so you can get rid of me and go on your own. (*Sighs.*) Well, that's gratitude for you. You little double-crosser! After all the years I've deprived myself of luxuries and riches just because I was sorry for you. I guarded you against the pitfalls of life at the expense of my career.

Shunned by society! Just because of you. You've dragged me into the gutter, made a bum out of me. My whole life ruined.

STAN: But, Ollie, I—

OLLIE: Don't but me. Pack your things to get out. I'm through with you. Don't ever talk to me again and if you ever see me—pretend you don't know me. Now pack up and get out. (*Picks up newspaper.* STAN *sorrowfully starts to pack his few belongings in a paper bag.* OLLIE *stares at newspaper, takes it big.*) (*Cut to closeup in newspaper: an advertisement in "Missing Heirs" column which reads:* ANYONE KNOWING THE WHEREABOUTS OF STANLEY LAUREL, PLEASE COMMUNICATE WITH DIBBS, DABS AND DOBBS, LAW OFFICES, NEW YORK, LONDON, PARIS, AND ROME.)

(OLLIE *immediately grabs his hat and coat, grabs* STAN *and pushes him out of the room. Dissolve to law office.* OLLIE *pushes* STAN *in, both out of breath.* STAN *bewildered, doesn't know what it's all about. A run through the streets if gags could be suggested.* OLLIE *introduces* STAN *to the lawyers. After introductions,* OLLIE *is told to leave the room as their business concerns* STAN *only;* OLLIE *leaves, sheepishly.* STAN *is advised that he has inherited $50,000, left to him by an uncle—on the one condition that* STAN *separates himself from* OLLIE—*who the uncle had met one time and took an instant dislike to. Uncle thinks* OLLIE *made a bum of* STAN *and dragged him in the gutter, and this*

will-proviso is to help STAN *start anew and to protect
him from the pitfalls of life which* OLLIE *has brought
him to.* STAN *doesn't know what to do so excuses himself to think it over. Takes the papers with him. He
exits to the anteroom where he finds* OLLIE *at a table.*
OLLIE *is burned up because of being dismissed from the
situation.)*

OLLIE: Well, what happened? (STAN *is silent.*) What's the
matter with you, can't you speak? (STAN *nods yes.*)
Well, why don't you say something?

STAN: You told me never to speak to you again.

OLLIE: That was socially, this is *business.* What happened?

STAN: I can't tell you—

OLLIE: And why can't you tell me?

STAN: Well, I don't know you.

OLLIE: (*Burns up.*) You mean you don't *want* to know me,
now that you have a lot of money. You want to forget
your old pal—throw me aside like an old cigar butt.
What gratitude! You little shrimp, let me see those papers. (*He grabs them from* STAN, *quickly reads amount
of inheritance and looks very pleased.*) Wonderful!
Fifty thousand dollars! Boy, can we go to town with
that. (*Continues to read, his face drops as he reads the
contents regarding the proviso. Looks very embarrassed.*)

STAN: Don't worry, Ollie. I won't sign it. What's fifty
thousand dollars? If it had been more, it would have
been different. But only fifty thousand dollars—he in-
sults my ignorance.

OLLIE: No, Stanley. Your uncle is probably right. Maybe I *am* to blame for you being so dumb and useless, and it's all been my fault. I'm sorry for all the unkind things I've said about you, and I think it's best for both of us to go our own way. And so we'll never see each other again.

STAN: How do you mean, Ollie?

OLLIE: I'll go that way, you go this way. (*He indicates the door and the window.* STAN *takes a look out the window; it's several stories up.*)

STAN: Not much use my signing this paper.

OLLIE: You must, Stanley, and when you are riding around in fine automobiles and living on the fat of the land, think of me once in a while, and remember I wasn't such a bad guy after all. If you ever happen to see me in your travels, you could wave to me. I'm sure your uncle wouldn't mind that. Well, come on, let's get the matter settled. (*Starts for door of lawyers' office.*)

STAN: But I'm not supposed to be with you any more!

OLLIE: I'll have to be there to agree that we'll never know each other any more.

STAN: (*At door of office, knocks.*) Yoo hoo! (*They go in.*)

The manuscript ends. From a note appended, it is clear that Stan inherits the money but because of a mixup in writing of the deed (one of the lawyers is Ben Turpin), the money only comes to Stan if Ollie *never* leaves his side, instead of the intended reverse. Moreover, the will also reads that Stan is to spend the inheritance on "the things that he loves most." Stan ponders this deeply and has to admit that the things he loves most are ice cream sodas. In typical literal obedience, Stan starts to consume ice cream sodas with his pal but by the end of the second day of their stupendous orgy, they are faced with the fact that at the current price of ice cream sodas, ten cents apiece, it seems unlikely they will ever be able to consume 500,000 sodas. Therefore, they give the rest of the money to an orphanage, and return to penniless and carefree vagabondage.

* * *

Chatting with Dick Van Dyke not long after Stan died, I asked this remarkable comedian, similar to Stan in many ways and virtually the only distinguished performer around these days able to get solid laughter from total pantomimic skill, just why he considered Stan the greatest of film comedians.

"Very simple," said Dick. "First of all because he got more *laughs* both as a performer and as a creator of gags, than almost anybody else in film comedy. Not even Chaplin gets as much laughter, pure *laughter,* as Stan does. Chaplin is great, a genius—but with Chaplin I can always see the technique showing. Lord knows it's great technique, and I admire it very much—but with Stan the technique never shows. *Never.* And that to me is proof that he is a better craftsman than Chaplin—an infinitely better craftsman."

To which I would add that the constituent elements of the comedy world of Stan Laurel, his essential hallmarks, are three in number. At the risk of delving into that kind of critical analysis Stan so much deplored, I will say briefly that the Laurel humor as seen in his films and as reflected in his sketches and the selections in this chapter evidence

a strain of high nonsense: ludicrousness presented warmly, solemnly, gently

positiveness: his work is irresistibly sanguine and celebratory of life

innocence: he wanted people to share in his sunny life view, a view in which guile had no place. His world is the world of the old English pantomime where everyone really *did* live happily ever after.

Stan had no "philosophy" of comedy, and he regarded any attempt to define one on anyone's part as a pretty amusing joke in itself. So let it rest—except for the following.

Stan:

"Never, for God's sake, ask me what makes people laugh. I just don't know. To get laughs you simply have to work hard all the time and learn how to do it in your bones. You can't do that until you get a lot of experience before live audiences. Audiences are strange things. I love them but sometimes they are hard to figure out. Sometimes they'll laugh at the damnedest things. I remember once going to a vaudeville show when I first arrived in New York. Vaudeville in 1910 in the States was sometimes mixed with a vulgar kind of non-sexual burlesque. At this show I went to, I was never so shocked in my life. A guy doing a tramp act comes on stage in a big hurry and spits out a mouthful of milk. His partner says, 'Where'd you get that?' and the tramp says, 'I just fell off a cow's teat!' (*Loud laughter.*) Now I ask you, is that humor? I laugh at it now because it is funny in a very crude way but that kind of humor really shocked me when I came here. In England you'd never see that kind of thing. I think English humor is a more gentle kind of humor over-all, but of course humor is humor anywhere. Actually in some ways English humor is even wilder than American humor, crazier somewhat—like the Goon Show on the B.B.C. That's typically English.

"Crazy humor was always my type of humor, but it's the quiet kind of craziness I like. The rough type of nut humor like the Marx Brothers I could never go for. I prefer the Dan Leno kind of thing. Above all, I particularly detest that smart-aleck, brash kind of humor that's based on insult—and I don't mean so much insult comedians themselves, although a few of *them* I don't care for—but the ones I really detest are the loud-mouthed guys on the talk shows who are so crazy about themselves. In comedy, the most important person is the person you're playing to—the person you're trying to make laugh. Too many young comedians these days forget that. A lot of them are up there performing in order to make *themselves* feel better, when it should be the other way around. And why don't some of them even try to use a little visual humor? They stand there and talk, talk, talk—and after a while I get the feeling that the only person they're really talking to is themselves. That's sad. That means they haven't learned the very first thing a comedian must learn— it is your audience that counts, not you."

"HE OF THE FUNNY WAYS"

STAN. JEFFERSON

Dude <u>and</u> Low Comedian

If Reply, please address

191

Stan's first calling card, circa 1906.

Six

In 1918 when Alice and Baldy Cooke, the other two corners of the Stan Jefferson Trio, reluctantly disbanded the act, they had the very strong feeling they had seen the last of Stan Laurel.

Alice Cooke:

"Baldy and I, of course, went on with our double act, working at it alone for over ten years before vaudeville started to die. That happened in the late 1920s, and so we came out to California just as lots of other ex-vaudevillians did, looking for a job in pictures. We had met Stan only once in that interval between 1918 and the end of vaudeville —just once briefly when Baldy and I were playing the Hippodrome in Los Angeles, and Stan was working as a single in pictures. Then some years later, when we came back to California after vaudeville died, Stan was teamed with Hardy and becoming famous at Roach's. As soon as Stan knew we were on the Coast and didn't have work, he insisted that we join him on the Roach lot, and so Baldy and I went to work, doing supporting parts in Laurel and Hardy and other Roach pictures for twenty years. Baldy and I played all kinds of funny little roles in the Laurel and Hardy pictures: for instance, Baldy's the man with the hose in *Perfect Day,* and an orderly in *County Hospital,* and a lot of other parts; I was a gypsy in *The Bohemian Girl,* Mother Hubbard in *Babes in Toyland,* and a night club patron in *Our Relations.*

"Stan was—and I'm telling nothing but the simple truth now—Stan was the kindest, most thoughtful, most generous and most loyal man I've ever met in my life. And so cheerful! Even when things were hard for him—and sometimes they were *very* hard for him, what with his marriage troubles, terrible troubles—he never complained. He was still the same lovely, smiling, funny man he had been all those years ago when we met during World War I. A lot of stars, when they get to be big, get big heads too. But never with Stan. He was always the same with us, and with all his old friends from the early days. Always that same sense of humor—always that wonderful laugh.

"As I said, he had some rough times. There were occasions when I bet he felt like crying—things got so bad for him with his marital difficulties. I knew all of his wives and, of course, Mae Laurel. Lois, the first wife, was a nice person, as I recall. Mae, of course, was a holy terror when Stan was starting out in pictures and it was a blessing she went back to Australia.*

"I was friendly with Virginia Ruth but she was hard on

* Mae Laurel returned to the United States in 1936. She promptly sued Stan for her property rights based on her tenure over a number of years as his common-law wife. The case was settled out of court with Mae receiving an undisclosed sum. After the encounter, Stan and Mae never met again. Thirty years later as I was interviewing Mae in the last year of her life, she said touchingly: "I still love him, you know."

Stan, in my opinion. When he married her, he built a beautiful three-bedroom house in Cheviot Hills. All Stan's life he
had wanted a big bathtub, a *sunken* bathtub, in the floor. So
for that Cheviot Hills bathroom, he took two of the bedrooms (they were all large) and made those two bedrooms
into a large bathroom. He couldn't have a sunken bathtub
because this was on the second floor, so he had a *raised*
sunken bathtub—you had to go up three steps to go into it.
He sure loved that bathtub. At the final divorce, the judge
awarded Virginia Ruth the house. She was very happy about
that but it proved to be a white elephant on her hands because it had only one bedroom.

"Then Stan's next wife. She was something! Illeana was
just incredible—that giant of a woman opposite little Stan.
That was something to see! And how mean she was to him.
All the time Stan was making big money he had those three
wives, and then just when he stopped making the big money,
he met Ida—the one (in my opinion) he should have married in the first place. I've always thought what a shame it
was that Ida, who was the best one in the world for Stan,
the one who took such good care of him, nursed him
through illness and bad luck—what a shame that Ida didn't
get the beautiful homes and luxurious living that all the
other wives got. Ida really deserved that. Not that she complained for a minute, though!"

Ida was approached in 1954 by Ralph Edwards to help
in documenting events in Stan's life for a proposed *This Is
Your Life* segment devoted to both Laurel and Hardy. She
was able to do this but at a considerable strain on her nerves.

Stan was almost always home and because he enjoyed answering the telephone, Ida's communications with the pro-
ducers of the show were severely limited. Finally she hit on
the device of having her brother serve as conduit from Edwards to herself. Her brother usually spoke to her in Russian,
and she replied to him in the same way, thereby allowing
her to give the television people what they wanted. Just
prior to the event, she had a most difficult time getting Stan
to get a haircut out of his usual time sequence.

The subterfuge used to get Laurel and Hardy to the
Knickerbocker Hotel where the program commenced was
the fortuitous arrival in Los Angeles of Bernard Delfont, the
man who had booked their British music hall tours. The
Hardys and the Laurels arrived at Delfont's rooms and were
having reunion cocktails when one door crashed open, spot-
lights flashed on and the snout of a television camera poked
in. Stan was shocked and Babe, thinking it was a holdup,
held his hand on his pocket. The unctuous Edwards tones
over the public address system reassured them, but on their
way to the studio, Stan confided his shock and disgust to
Ida. Consequently, during the program he uttered less than
a dozen words, polite words, but as he said to me afterwards,
"I was damned if I was going to put on a free show for
them." One part of him very much resented the program
because Laurel and Hardy were then very available for television work, and Mr. Edwards was getting some pretty
potent talent for nothing. But above all, Stan was repulsed
by the disorder of the enterprise. He never made a public
appearance without extensive and meticulous rehearsal. To

be thrust helter-skelter into a program of unceasing (and for the most part very dull) surprises was not his cup of tea.

Notwithstanding, he was gravely courteous during the program, and was most gracious to Mr. Edwards. Edwards during the proceedings announced that there was going to be a big party afterwards for all the guests. His tone implied that he, as host, was looking forward to this hot-diggetty affair at the Knickerbocker with unbounded eagerness. Stan's one and thoroughly satisfying laugh of the evening came when Mr. Edwards failed to show up. "It was a farce, the whole damned thing," Stan told me later. "Just like a bloody home movie!" And then conscious that he had given a pretty satisfying description of the program, he relaxed into that delightful laugh of his which I have always characterized, with great affection, as a refined horse laugh. Stan could never stay angry for very long, and almost always his dissatisfaction with a matter was either erased or ameliorated by his discovering some fundamental absurdity about it which triggered his healing laughter.

And above all other things that warmed him was the comforting presence of Ida. In the last decade of his life, Stan wrote his old friend of English music hall days, Wee Georgie Wood, and said, "They say I'm not a millionaire any more. They're crazy. I've got Ida." She was able to cushion many of the mundane pressures which came to Stan in his last years, and if she was not able to share in the riches of his palmy days, she was present in 1961 when he received his most prized gift in life—the special Oscar awarded him by the Academy of Motion Picture Arts and Sciences. Ida learned certain nursing skills which were vital to sustain him in his diabetic regimen. Additionally, she had to extend herself physically on many occasions to help him move about after the stroke which felled him on April 25, 1955. He was not seriously incapacitated despite the severe stiffness which afflicted his left side, but he was very conscious of a slight slurring in his speech. Consequently, in the first year after the stroke, he tended not to answer the telephone as much as he used to. Gradually, the slurring disappeared and he returned to a heavy use of the telephone. He insisted that his number be listed in the telephone book on the grounds that anyone who really wanted to talk to him was so entitled, at least for a few minutes.

This openness of approach he extended even to his very door. It became known to various sightseer bus operators that Stan lived at the Oceana Hotel, Ocean Avenue, in Santa Monica, and they broadcast this information during the tours. As a result and not infrequently, Mr. and Mrs. Just Folks would appear at the Laurel door with the hearty news that they had just heard that Mr. Laurel lived here, they just loved Mr. Laurel and would it be possible to meet Mr. Laurel? It was a request never refused despite the fatigue it caused Stan, and his visitors found him unfailingly gracious. On one of the rare days when he was not feeling up to snuff, a girl who called from the hotel desk asking if she might meet him was told by Ida that he was resting in bed. It was not until Stan received a letter of regret from the young lady a few days later that he discovered her name—Leslie Caron.

After his stroke, he went out very little because in the early phase of his affliction one foot tended to drag a little. So it was that he saw an awful lot of television—in several senses of "awful lot." He had favorite shows: he loved the fights and liked *What's My Line?* He enjoyed comedy shows except those which featured comedians who were glib, aggressive, and self-appreciative. One of the game shows he watched was *Password,* a program in which contestants must guess the identity of words only the audience and the gamemaster know. This latter was (and in 1973 *still* was) Allen Ludden, a notably uncolorful master of ceremonies whose principal duties are handing cards to contestants, listening to their guesses, commiserating politely when they lose, smiling and crinkling his eyes cutely when they win.

The network and press designations of Ludden as the "star" of the show struck Stan as hilarious. "What are he and people like him stars *of?*" he asked me one day. "Who made them stars? In my day, a star was a person who entertained you so damned much it almost lifted you out of your seat." Stan had no resentment of Ludden—he simply found him somewhat incredible. References to Ludden and peers as "television personalities" gave Stan much amusement because, as nearly as he could detect, Ludden and peers had no discernible personality at all. "These people aren't even bad talents. They are simply non-talents," Stan said, and although he did not fault these non-talents for embracing their star billing, he was irritated at a system which permitted this at a time when skilled performers were out of work. "I can name ten good supporting players from the Roach lot who could pull cards from a machine, read them off and also make you fall down laughing at the same time—but instead we get Mr. Ludden."

But because Stan was not a negative person, irritations of this sort did not linger. Indeed, after a time, the banalities he saw on television became rather like old feeble-minded friends; one greeted them pleasantly, passed the time of day with them politely, even developed a kind of affection for them. I watched Stan once as he sat in great good humor looking at a game show of particularly strident inanity. The "host" of this horror was typical of his breed—an organ-voiced, gleaming toothed, self-loving nonentity who whooped up audience enthusiasm with exhilarating cries of "Keep going, atta boy!" to contestants who bounced balloons on their chins and tittered endlessly. Stan watched this scrambling, screaming grab bag of banality with undiluted pleasure. I thought for one horrified moment that he was really enjoying it. And so he was—but not in the way I guessed. "How nice," he said to me with deep sincerity, "that so many people get such a hell of a charge out of so little."

Although he did not work at it every day by any means, the act of composing ideas for gags and then structuring them was a part of his world. He talked with Babe on the telephone frequently, and in the first stages of Stan's illness Babe came over for lunch one day. As he sat down, smiling mischievously at his old partner, Babe said, "Well, here's another fine mess you've gotten *yourself* into!" They laughed uproariously. Despite his stroke, Stan felt sanguine about his performing future—until Babe's stroke on September 12,

1956. This was a heavily debilitating one, and after a hospital stay, Babe was taken home and went through a severe period of multiple illnesses. His convalescence was greatly hampered by a gall bladder attack but surgical relief for this problem was prevented by a newly found heart condition. The stroke triggered an aphasia which made consecutive thought almost impossible. However, when Stan came to visit him, Babe recognized his old partner without difficulty although he was unable to speak to him. It was a meeting of particularly affecting poignancy not only because it was their last but because these two great masters of pantomime spoke to each other for an hour principally in gesture. Stan's most vivid memory of that visit was a silent facial and bodily movement from Babe which said, "Look at me. Isn't this appalling?" Lucille Hardy and Ida left the two men alone for a moment as they said goodbye.

Babe died on August 7, 1957.

Stan:

"He was like a brother to me. We seemed to sense each other. Funny, we never really got to know each other personally until we took the tours together. When we made pictures, it was all business even though it was fun. Between pictures we hardly saw each other. His life outside the studio was sports —and my life was practically all work, even after work was over. I loved editing and cutting the pictures, something he wasn't interested in. But whatever I did was tops with him. There was never any argument between us, ever. I hope wherever he is now that he realizes how much people loved him."

Stan was forbidden by his doctor to attend the funeral. "It's just as well," Stan said. "I might have said or done something funny to hide the hurt—and Babe would have understood. But I don't think others might have." With his partner gone, Stan mourned deeply until he found a creative form of solace: he created new Laurel and Hardy gags.

Thereafter the high point of his day became the arrival of mail. He enjoyed going down to the desk of the Oceana to get it, and it grew into a ritual: dressing up a bit to go down to the lobby, jollying the clerk as he received the mail, taking the elevator back to his second floor apartment overlooking the ocean, waving to the people in the Oceana swimming pool, and then sitting at his desk to read, and in many cases to answer immediately, the mail. Like his approach to comedy, Stan's desk was a model of order—everything in its place: stationery, typewriter, paper clips, letter opener, all neatly arranged. Interestingly, he had what can really be called a passion for the articles on and in his desk. He loved making special trips just to buy a paper punch or a special kind of stamp or a new kind of stationery.

"If I had never been a comedian," he said once, "I would really have enjoyed owning a stationery store, running it myself. I don't know why that is, but outside of my work, my favorite thing to do is just go out and visit stationery stores." Although he was uncertain why he enjoyed visiting these shops so much, I believe the one element common to these places, their myriad product and Stan was a compact neatness. Stan had a high sense of order, a strong feeling for detail, and everything-in-its-place was as true of his stationery, his impeccable linen and clothing, and his handwriting as it was of his work preparations. "Funny—Babe was very neat, too," he said. "That was another thing we had in common."

In working at his mail, Stan was able to answer the usual daily quota he received but on special occasions—his birthday, Babe's death, a hospital stay—letters arrived by the thousands. These letters came from every strata of society and every part of the world. He received pictures of new babies from doting parents, and one gentleman in South Africa periodically sent pictures of his ostrich. Stan was never quite sure how to answer the ostrich fancier—but he did, faithfully. He was as punctilious and thoroughgoing in his replies to the unknowns as he was to the knowns among his admirers. Among the latter, and there were many of them, the following will serve as samples.

Puissance	*Purveyors*
without	*to the*
hauteur	*trade*

GRAYBAR THEATRICAL PRODUCTION CO., INC.
Sole Makers of Bob and Ray Stuff

April 3, 1961

Stan Laurel,
Santa Monica, Calif.

Dear Mr. Laurel:

Have just finished the McCabe book, and couldn't resist writing to express how much enjoyment you and Ollie have given me over the years.

I should say how much enjoyment you have given *us,* since I am half of the Bob and Ray team, and if our humor has ever come within a mile of yours, it's because of our life-long devotion to, and study of, Laurel and Hardy.

You are, I understand, still deluged with fan mail—and I imagine the book has increased it—so I won't dwell overlong on your time. Likewise, you have had accolades from just about every one of the greats in show business, so ours is but a wee small voice added to the rest.

Perhaps, however, you do like to hear, now and then, from those who, apart from being just fans, truly appreciate the extent of perfection you achieved in your work, and who will always revere the greatness of Stan and Ollie.

In one word, "Thanks!"

Sincerely,

Bob Elliott

Stan replied:

April 12, 1961

Dear Bob Elliott:

Thanks for your very nice letter. I appreciated very much your kind sentiments so graciously expressed.

Am pleased to know you enjoyed the L. and H. book and found it interesting.

I had a hemorrhage in my left eye recently, so the doctor advised me to avoid reading and writing for a while—so please pardon me for being brief.

My kindest regards and good wishes to Ray and self.

Sincerely, always:

Stan Laurel

In 1973, Bob Elliott told me: "Laurel and Hardy got to both Ray and me early in our lives and we've never lost enthusiasm for their films no matter how often we've seen them. I think since we've teamed up we've probably studied them inasmuch as their being a team was akin to our being a team. That's kind of confusing; what I think I mean is that the technique of team comedy is much different than the single stand-up variety and because of that we're more interested in team performance and Laurel and Hardy are, for us, the greatest."

The eye difficulty mentioned in the letter to Bob Elliott also forced Stan to again be uncharacteristically brief in his reply (since lost) to this letter:

> Los Angeles
> 3 June 1961
>
> Dear Mr. Laurel:
> I meant to write you immediately after you received your so richly deserved recognition from the Academy, but was unable to trace your address immediately and then got caught up in my work and forgot. But now someone has got it for me.
> Unfortunately I leave in about four days time, returning to England, and I have looping, etc., to do at the studio, otherwise I would have loved to have called on you. But I will try to reach you on the telephone before I go.
> Your Academy Award gave such tremendous pleasure to everyone—but it was a particular joy to me. For me you have always been and always will be one of the truly greats. I think one of my earliest ambitions was to emulate you in some way, and certainly one of my first

successes (although a modest one) in the theatre was playing Sir Andrew Aguecheek in Shakespeare's *Twelfth Night* rather on the lines you might have played it. I was only twenty-three at the time and I think the copying of you was unconscious—but it was certainly noticed by the critics, and that goes to show how much I had absorbed and loved your work.

Anyway, this brief letter is just to pay homage to a great comedian and to wish you all happiness and the hope that I may meet you some day.

Yours sincerely,
Alec Guinness

Stan was always particularly touched by praise from people in his profession although the awards he received were always accepted (albeit gratefully) with a sense of quiet fun. His Academy Award statuette he dubbed "Mr. Clean," and on the occasion when Screen Actors Guild presented him with a beautiful inscribed crystal bowl, he felt properly honored but also, and inevitably, amused. "I don't know what it's for," he said later. "For being a nice guy, or some goddamned thing. (*Loud laughter.*) But it's very nice. It's like an eye wash bowl grown up. I'd have been better off with a cement mixer, but I *do* deeply appreciate it."

Show business guests at the Santa Monica apartment were always asked to autograph a visitors' book which Stan enjoyed keeping. A random sampling from the book reveals that comedians dominate the visitor list but others came too:

God bless—and may I always be allowed to sit in your chair—even if it's a breakdown!

Jack Carter

The Comedy World of Stan Laurel

To Dear Stan—with my greatest admiration.
                                    Peter Sellers
                                    June 1964

Dear Stan—

When I used to run your two-reelers in the only
theatre in the college town where I used to attend school,
I certainly never hoped to have the honor of presenting
you with an award from the Screen Actors Guild. It is
one of the important moments I'll always remember. God
bless you!

                                    Dana Andrews

To Stan—always my idol—and my friend for many years.
This is an honor I'll always remember.
                        Rex Van
                        (Moran of "Moran and Mack—
                        The Two Black Crows.")

                To Stan—the King—
                All my best—your No. 1 Fan—
                                    Ken Murray

                To Stan—
                For all my life, my favorite.
                                    Dick Martin
                                    Rowan and Martin
                                    1-9-62

To Mr. Stan Laurel—
This has been the thrill of my life! God bless you.
                                    Dick Van Dyke

There are few giants. You are a giant among giants. My great admiration for you and what you have contributed to this wonderful profession of ours!

Danny Kaye

To *the* but *THE* greatest of them all—
Bless you!

Patsy Kelly

"Golden lads and girls all must—"
Ah, Stan—but the fun we've had!

Dennis King

The tenor of Stan's life went its even way more evenly as his final years commenced. He had a special feeling for where he lived. When not watching television or answering mail, he enjoyed looking out over the ocean long minutes at a time. A friend asked him once why he seemed to be watching it intently. "Simple," said Stan. "I'm watching to see if submarines will ever surface. None ever do, but it sure as hell keeps me busy!" This pleasantry hid the fact that Stan loved the sea with devotion. In his moneyed days, his only recreation was deep sea fishing, and he once owned a fishing yacht which the government needed and purchased from him during World War II.

Stan had a talent for sleeping. Next to the Oceana Hotel was an old house long past its prime, and one very early morning it burned down. There was much coming and going on the street: honking cars, fire engines and police cars with screaming sirens roaring up and down. The noise aroused

Ida and she looked out at the scene below, directly under their apartment. The din was horrendous. A large crowd gathered quickly; everyone in the neighborhood had been awakened. Except Stan. Long after it was over, he woke up and Ida told him about all the fuss. In telling someone about it later, Stan said, "Yes, I slept through the whole damned thing. When I die, they'll really know I'm dead."

For recreation in addition to television, he listened to old recordings of great British music hall artists (he had a notable collection), and when a persistently hemorrhaging eye permitted, he read a bit. One time I noticed him reading what was obviously a playscript. This play, I discovered, was the focus of Stan's only, and very vaguely conceived, desire to play in the legitimate theatre. He gave me the script to read. It was *Moon Over Mulberry Street*, by Nicholas Cosentino. I found it unremarkable dramatically but pleasant; it was what years ago used to be known as a "good stock show," a play which offered a fairly small number of characters placed in a single setting and involved in a homey, down-to-earth plot. *Moon Over Mulberry Street's* plot is highly predictable once one encounters the leading characters: a poor, young Italian-American lawyer who falls in love with a Park Avenue girl. He becomes bitter when she leaves him. But the little neighborhood girl (the neighborhood is the Italian section of Greenwich Village), who has been hanging around "for acts and acts," one critic said, turns out to be just the girl for him.

This play, which introduced Cornel Wilde to the theatre, had a brief run in New York in September 1935. The critics were devastating. John Mason Brown called it "dull and amateurish"; Richard Lockridge said the author showed conclusive proof of his lack of aptitude for the theatre; Arthur Pollack said the play was "merely without merit of any kind." "Any kind" is very unjust, but it *is* a slight piece. What interested me was that there was not a single character in it which fitted Stan Laurel. Why, then, was he so taken with the play, and how did he expect to fit into it?

Stan:

"I know it's no great shakes as a play. But it's got a very nice, warm feeling about it. The people in it are very nice, warm people. As for my part in it, that would have to be written. The way the play came to me was interesting. It came to me very directly. I was on the train going from New York to Los Angeles one time, and just after I had settled into my compartment I felt a nudge from an object in the corner of my seat. I reached down and from under the seat cushion I pulled out this copy of *Moon Over Mulberry Street*. I didn't have very much to read with me, so I started to look at it just to pass the time of day.

"The more I read, the more interested I got in that family, that Italian family, and all their troubles. Sure, the plot line is very obvious; you know what's going to happen. But then you know what's going to happen in a lot of good stories and plays. It's not so important *what* happens as *how* it happens, how human and interesting the people are. I never forgot this play, and from time to time I take it out and read it again. While Babe was living I would never appear without him, of course, but after he was gone once in a while I'd think about doing the play. I don't think that'll ever happen now [1960], but if I should miraculously get my health back again, I'm at least in the mood on occasion to contact the author for permission for me to rewrite the play to include the Stanley character. I think a lot of good, gentle humor—and even some pretty interesting drama—could come from having Stanley come into that family's life, get mixed up with them, creating some good laughs—but then ultimately straightening things out O.K. for the family, clearing up their troubles, and then leaving them just as he came—out of the nowhere, mysteriously."

Stan had not taken the plotting of the action of *Moon Over Mulberry Street* beyond this point, and shortly after this time he also came to the determination that out of respect to the memory of Laurel and Hardy he would never again perform as a single, even if his health allowed. The interesting thing to me about the *Moon Over Mulberry Street* matter was the revelation that his creative faculties were not only unfaltering but had actually taken a more serious and adventuresome turn. Stan never had the opportunity to display his total ability as an actor but that he was capable of a penetrating wryness and a haunting pathos I never doubted. In those very rare moments when he talked seriously, his superbly expressive face would take on far-ranging casts of expression. One need only look at the photograph of Stan in his dressing room between performances of "Birds of a Feather" in this book to see how his face in repose reflected a soft, deep pensiveness. That face which was trained principally to register clownish vacuity could also display wide extensions of emotion.

In the years following his stroke, Stan's health, except for his final year and one brief hospital stay, gradually improved. The hospital visit was the result of a diabetic upset and it was disturbing to Stan not only in that it was intrusive on his time but also in that the hospital, a Seventh-day Adventist establishment in San Fernando Valley, did not serve meat to its patients. "I'm going to start chewing on my foot if this keeps up," he told a visitor. One visitor he expected did not appear. This was a famous comedian who not long before had expressed, during a visit at the Oceana, an undying affection for Stan and all his works. This gentleman failed to show up during the hospital stay at a time when Stan needed company, especially company of the kind the comedian could have so easily provided. Some time after this, Ida learned that this gentleman did not want to go to the hospital because it would have caused him "too much pain" to see Stan prostrate.

One comedian able to bear up under the sight of Stan prostrate was Jack Oakie who, although a total stranger to Stan, made a considerable point in coming to entertain a man who both loved and needed entertainment. Oakie, with the ebulliently robust charm which characterized his film work, gave Stan a memorable few hours.

In 1963, it became apparent to me, based principally on the volume and the tenor of the mail which Stan was receiving and similar mail coming to me following the publication of *Mr. Laurel and Mr. Hardy*, that Laurel and Hardy buffs were not only legion but needed a focus for their deep love of the films, an opportunity to share that love intra-murally. After discussing the matter with Stan, he approved my founding the Sons of the Desert, a group deriving its name from the 1933 Laurel and Hardy film of that title in which the boys give their loyalties to a national lodge. The film gently satirizes national social brotherhoods, and in permitting the founding of our group, Stan made only one proviso. The group *must*, he insisted, maintain at all times a "half-assed dignity." The group, now boasting twenty Tents or scion societies in various American cities, has maintained precisely that dignity in high and persequent devotion. Indeed the half is more frequently three-quarters, a development which would not have displeased Stan at all, in my view.*

There had been one group of Laurel and Hardy devotees in existence before the Sons of the Desert. This was the Laurel and Hardy Club of Duarte, California, which main-tained a clubhouse where they showed the films on a regular basis. A few of the members visited Stan weekly, and he much enjoyed their company, entertaining them with de-lightful stories and hearty badinage. The Club, anxious to repay the wonderful hospitality, found various sources of in-come in order to buy Stan a gift which they hoped might

* As of 1989, there were over a hundred Tents worldwide, including 68 in the United States. Those wishing to know the location of the Tent nearest them, or to form a Tent in their area, may contact Scott MacGillivray at P.O. Box 1358, Brookline MA 02146.

prove a particular pleasure for him. The gift was something he did indeed deeply appreciate — a handsome color television set. But, of course, he found the presentation of the gift an irresistible occasion for a gag. As the members of the Club stood eagerly around the color set at the moment he first saw it, he said, "Gee, thanks *so* much. It's wonderful!" He paused, and added soberly, "But I guess you didn't know I was color blind, did you?" The group's consternation was at once joyously relieved by his ringing laughter.

Stan had a daily telephone call which never varied. This was from his lawyer and long-time confidant, Ben Shipman, who in earlier years had been business manager of Hal Roach Studios. Stan and Ben counted a day wasted when one or the other did not tell a bright new story usually compounded of the gravest nonsense. They tried studiously to break each other up and usually succeeded. One of the serious matters they discussed from time to time was Stan's finances. Stemming from the time when he was unemployed after the Roach period, Stan had a certain degree of apprehension about his monetary status but, as it turned out, he need not have worried. Financially, because of prudent investments made by Ben Shipman years before, Stan was secure and was able to leave his widow secure.

It is the only blessing I can think of in connection with Stan's death that he was not alive to witness the (to me) incredible assault on his estate made by his former wife, Virginia Ruth Laurel, an action that distressed Stan's doughty widow considerably. The suit contested Stan's will, a two-page document dated November 3, 1947, which bequeathed his entire estate valued (in usual legal phraseology) as "in excess of $10,000" to his widow, Ida. The document by implication acknowledged the deep devotion to Stan given by Ida, a devotion extended past his lifetime when she became the keeper of his flame.

In contesting the will, Virginia Ruth contended that she was still legally married to Stan, despite the divorce she obtained from him in Nevada on April 30, 1946. This was easily disproved. At this time a contest was also filed, alleging that Stan was "not of sound and disposing mind and memory" at the time he made the will. This, too, was (in legal parlance) "voluntarily dismissed" by the court. It is irony of a supreme degree that this would have been selected as one of the key reasons to contest the will. Not long before he died, Stan was enumerating the ailments that age had brought to him, and he said to Ida, "I guess about the only thing I've got left in me that's one hundred per cent sound is my heart." "No, my darling," she said. "It's your brain. That wonderful, witty brain." She was, need one say it, unarguably correct.

In the very last years of his life, Stan came to see two people more frequently than any others, and it is, I think, a very revealing indication of his wide interests that one man was a technician in the film industry, the other an actor of strong intellectual bent. Stan usually saw them at different times. Joe Finck, a film cutter, almost always came Wednesday nights, frequently with friends from the Duarte fan club. Booth Colman, brilliant character actor in many Hollywood films, came on other occasions.

Joe Finck:

"The first and lasting memory I have of Stan is of his courtesy. I have never in all my life met a man who was so unfailingly courteous. Even if he was watching a TV show he liked very much and someone he didn't even know came over unexpectedly, off would go the set at once. The visitor was always first. We used to sit and chat about all kinds of things—anything under the sun. Those of us who were in the Laurel and Hardy Club loved to hear him talk of the way he did the pictures, of course, and of the little incidents surrounding the making of the pictures. I remember him once describing very vividly how he and his double, Ham Kinsey, were taking a pleasant few minutes rest between shots on one of the two-reelers. They were sitting in the dressing room, having some drinks, having just a grand time. 'Boy, this is the life!' Stan said to Ham. And just as he said it, the ground started to tremble, they heard a strange kind of noise, and the whole building started to shake. It was the great California earthquake of the mid-1930s! Stan was always proud of his timing, he said.

"Of course that great sense of humor always kept us in stitches. He commiserated with one of our members, Bob Stowell, when several color slides Bob took of Stan didn't turn out. 'Unfortunately, I'm not too photogenic as a model,' Stan said. 'I'm just not the type. I'm a better subject for oils —Crisco, for preference!'

"Even when he was initially troubled by his stroke, he retained a great deal of his performing skills. I can remember when some lively music was playing (Stan loved the old time popular songs and nostalgic music), he would do a soft-shoe dance, seated. Then he would do that great pantomime trick of rolling his derby down from his head, along his extended arm and into his hand.

"The greatest fun, though, was watching his old movies with him on television. He never watched himself, only Hardy—and Hardy just made him break up all over the place. It was so wonderful seeing him laugh so uproariously at his old partner. For one thing, in addition to Hardy's great gifts as a comedian, Stan loved his professionalism. Stan could never understand people in his business—and there are lots of them—who weren't professionals at heart, or who didn't take advantage of the fullest opportunities offered them to do their very best.

"For instance, one man who was interested in seeking Stan out as a source of gag inspiration, used to come up with his crew to talk with Stan for hours at a time—sometimes until three in the morning. And all that time Stan would be giving this man advice—advice which the man never seemed to take. That was hard for Stan to understand.

"Stan, of course, was a real craftsman in every way, and at the end of his life when he didn't have his films to edit, he found great pleasure in working over tape recordings. He had an amazing versatility at this—with the splicer, et cetera. He never recorded his own voice. He was fondest of recording old English music hall songs from disc records he owned and then sending the tapes as gifts to friends of his.

"Above all, there was his wonderful laugh. One time he laughed so hard that he almost had a spasm, a real attack. But he pulled out of it (we were really worried). He told us not to worry. 'The day I can't laugh any more, dig me a hole and bury me,' he said. And I'll never forget the time when we were watching Dick Powell's funeral on television. Stan turned to me, and he said, 'If anyone at my funeral has a long face, I'll never speak to them again!'"

Booth Colman met Stan in 1947 and except for periodic road tours was a weekly visitor at the Laurels. Of all Stan's friends in the later years, Booth knew him the best and saw most deeply into the man within and his functions as an artist. It is for this reason that I let Booth's memories of him stand as what I consider the finest ultimate assessment.

Booth Colman:

"He was always, of course, a delightful man, full of great fun and unending anecdote. It was difficult at times to get serious with him but he did have his serious moments. However, the underlying feeling was—one mustn't get unduly serious. Very often if we were discussing some political topic of the day, a serious book, or a play, and I might get carried away for the moment, he would always have a way of bringing me back by interpreting something in the zany, offbeat way that his screen character might. He looked at life in this manner.

"His early experiences, at least from the time he went into

vaudeville seemed to follow that mode: he looked on the bright side of things, and would always find the silly side, the laughable side, in almost every situation. I think probably that stood him in very good stead a number of times in his career.

"In his most successful days when there was a great deal of money, his natural kindness made him a kind of permanent host. Those were the Fort Laurel days at Canoga Park, and I gathered from what he told me that he had open house most of the time—well stocked bar, and all that kind of thing. More than once I heard him say, 'In Hollywood, today you're everyone's host; but tomorrow you're nobody's guest.' I think he took it very hard—harder than he cared to admit, that after the decline of the team's career he was not sought after.

"But being sought after *did* come eventually, toward the end of his life when he was more or less a living legend and there had been a new generation of comedians—many of them intellectual comedians—and other people, who recognized his great worth and merit. But among a number of his contemporaries he was *not* sought after. In a way, perhaps, he wasn't at his best with his colleagues socially. He enjoyed being with people who were *not* necessarily in the business, and this was a great blessing in his later life when so many of his audience—non-professionals all—sought him out.

"There was, of course, that fallow period when he and Babe still had their health, were eager and able to work, but were (it seems) studiously avoided by many people. One reason they did not get offers during that period when they were still able to work was because of Louella Parsons's unofficial blacklisting of them. When this curious lady had her Hollywood Hotel radio program in the 1930s, the only paid performer on her show was Dick Powell, who was getting $5,000 a week. The stars who were invited to appear on her program *contributed* their services—willingly or unwillingly.

"She was, of course, an enormous power at that time, and those were the days before A.F.T.R.A., the radio performers' union. She wanted 'her boys' (as she always termed Stan and Babe) on her show, and she telephoned Stan personally. Very courageously he mentioned something about a fee, and she was outraged. Took very real umbrage at the question and at him. He told me that for years after, she never mentioned Laurel and Hardy in her column unless it was something derogatory. I think that had a very real effect on their waning career.

"Then, too, Stan was the first to admit that a motion picture comedy team had a certain life span of popularity. Stan thought that span was about ten years or so, but I know if they had been free agents during their heyday, they would have been in a much more desirable position. Roach for years kept their contracts staggered, and he was always able to talk Babe into this. Stan fought the arrangement until finally he was able to convince Babe that their greatest interest lay in their controlling their own destinies. But by that time it was too late, and so they rode out their plushest years on the Roach lot.

"Stan's social life, unlike Babe's, was extremely restricted.

Stan told me one story of his being, uncharacteristically, at a rather gala Hollywood party one night, having a few drinks. The next day Stan remarked to his then wife (not Ida) that John Barrymore who was very much in the news at the time must be quite a character, very much worth meeting. His wife replied, 'What do you mean, want to meet him? You got tipsy with him last night at the party.' This would be typical of a man who simply didn't meet people. He very rarely went to gatherings. He just didn't crave that sort of thing. I think he felt very ill at ease in a large group.

"I was with him on several occasions at testimonial dinners at The Masquers Club when he was forced by certain circumstances to attend, and when he had to greet the occasional V.I.P., he was clearly not in his element. I think he had bitter memories, or memories at least that annoyed him. I remember once his meeting Jack Warner in the vestibule of The Masquers when they exchanged a word or two. I had heard him speak of Warner before—an attractive contract he had once offered Stan, and which mysteriously evaporated. The Warners didn't even have the courtesy to tell him that the deal was not going to be put through. They didn't offer the respect which Stan, rightly, felt was due him. So—seeing Warner that time stirred up that unhappy memory, and Stan was courteous as he was unfailingly, but I know the memory rankled. The offhanded way people were so frequently treated always annoyed Stan.

"Socially, Stan and Babe were, of course, not close. They were quite different men obviously. Babe liked his Lakeside

Country Club—with the golf he could play so well, and the card games that were so much a part of his life. Whereas Stan didn't go anywhere really, unless forced to. His off-camera life in the productive years by and large were spent in the cutting room and previewing and recutting the pictures, timing the laughs, that sort of thing. Like Chaplin, he was an all-around craftsman to his fingertips.

"So in a certain sense Stan and Babe were not close—except, of course, in their work. There the connection between the two was telepathic. Theirs was an ensemble playing which few artists ever achieve.

"Stan was not a great reader although he did enjoy collecting books on English music hall. Some of those people he enjoyed as Chaplin did: Dan Leno, Little Tich, Vesta Tilley, Vesta Victoria and the like. He had a standing order at Foyle's in London for such books, and would receive every one that came out. But his intellectual interests were limited. He took a certain interest in politics. He regarded himself as a liberal Democrat although he was never an American citizen. He admired FDR and JFK enormously, also Adlai Stevenson. He was devoid of *any* prejudice. Indeed he could never understand racial prejudice. This was a reflection of his deep and innate kindness.

"He loved amateur shows, and never missed the Major Bowes and similar amateur hours. He enjoyed seeing people trying to get up an act, trying to develop an act. It reminded him so much of his early days as a young professional in Scotland. Stan, of course, also liked a number of the younger comedians, among them Dick Van Dyke and Jerry Lewis—both men who loved Stan's work. Once Jerry Lewis offered Stan a very handsome salary to simply read scripts and make suggestions but Stan who was certainly far from being a rich man did not accept. He felt that he could not work in that way with Lewis because their styles were so completely disparate. He said he would rather have Lewis's friendship than risk the chance of argument with him.

"Once, Stan broke one of his own personal rules of very long standing: he actually went out to a movie theatre to see another comedian. Stan set up this rule for two reasons. First, he thought professional courtesy between comedians was best served only by mutual invitation to see each other's work, a thing rarely done. He preferred to see other comedians only when invited. He knew this was a very old-fashioned view but he adhered to it. Second, he anticipated disliking some comedians and would rather not have this circumstance arise. Of course there were times when he could not help seeing other comedians' work, as on television. But, on this occasion, when he broke his rule and went to a theatre to see another comedian, it was to go to a Jerry Lewis film. The visit was a mistake. Stan didn't appreciate the film, didn't understand it, didn't think it was funny—and all in spite of the fact that he had great affection for Lewis. It was a style which confused Stan. He thought the Lewis style was too aimless and chaotic and lacked the basis of a permanent character—a defined character—that being the school of thought to which Stan subscribed.

"Stan, of course, was most fortunate in possessing the wife he did. Ida was the most understanding and solicitous of women, and she certainly had to put up with a great deal in respect to privacy. Many times the bell would ring and Mr. and Mrs. Poop Face from Punkin Corners would appear, just showing up to meet their favorite actor. So Stan would invite them in, have them sit down and then, in response to their questions, repeat for the ten-thousandth time how he met Hardy, et cetera, et cetera. Not that he minded very much. In fact he seemed to thrive on it. Ida, of course, in order to maintain any privacy under these conditions, simply had to withdraw into their bedroom and close the door. A remarkable and generous-hearted person.

"Stan was in every way an artist, and he knew great artistry when he saw it. He had never seen Garbo in films, only when they were rerun on television. She impressed him very much. Indeed serious acting always did impress him. And great plays. I remember his watching *Hamlet* on television and never once making fun of it—and Stan was born to make fun.

"In summing up his artistry, I think he had only one difficulty—he was not ever his own boss in any depth. Easily the equal of Chaplin in equipment, Stan could never fully orchestrate his own genius because of never having absolute control of his films after the splendid years of the 1930s. And yet how wonderful he was despite these restrictions—and how much laughter he gave the world!

"In sum, a great and a very *good* man."

Thus Booth Colman, and an evaluation to which I subscribe in every particular.

If any further confirmation of Stan's innate goodness is needed after the evidences offered by the people in these pages who knew him well, it would come in the form of an envelope—a bulky, battered envelope, unmarked—which Ida and I found in his files after his death. Ida knew Stan's files very well. They contained much of his old correspondence, legal and contractual papers, and of course the file of gags discussed in a previous chapter. But this bulky envelope, stuck in one corner of a file drawer, she could not recall. The high likelihood is that Stan wanted to keep the contents purely to himself. What was in the envelope constitutes living documentation of Stan Laurel's deep and abiding sense of charity, of his unremitting love for his fellow man.

The envelope was chock-full of thank-you letters, and it recorded how through the many years of his life he had contributed extensively not only to hundreds of charities but to many individuals—many clearly unknown to him—who had written for financial help. I forbear quoting some of these letters of fervent thanks because there is the risk of sobsisterism descending over what were natural impulses of a generous and giving man. Moreover, dwelling on it unduly, or dwelling on it at *all*, would have genuinely disturbed him, I believe. Suffice to say these letters verify in depth that Stan Laurel spoke not as sounding brass or tinkling cymbal.

He died on February 23, 1965, of a heart attack.

How endearingly typical of him that his last words were a joke! When the nurse preparing a hypodermic was working briskly at her task, Stan said, very solemnly, "I wish I was skiing now." The nurse, intrigued, said, "Oh, are you a skier, Mr. Laurel?" "No," he said, breaking into his best smile, "but better be doing that than having these needles stuck into me." He died a few minutes later. It was a blessing death took him when it did because he was also afflicted with cancer of the palate. Ida and his doctor had been able to keep that knowledge from him, but it would not have been long before severe pain became his daily lot.

In accordance with his specific request, he was cremated. "I don't see why, with space for humans already so severely limited, that the dead should be allowed to take up so much space," he said on occasion.

His funeral was held at 3 P.M. on February 26, 1965, at Church of the Hills, Hollywood Hills. Dick Van Dyke spoke the eulogy, a moving and—as Stan would have wished—a cheerful one. Following the service, as the mourners (how Stan would have made a gag out of that word!) moved out of the church, Buster Keaton, who at first hand had worked with and had himself been among the finest comedians of his age, spoke to Andy Clyde, walking beside him. "Stan was the greatest," he said. "Even greater than Chaplin. Charlie was second. And don't let anyone fool you about *that*." Keaton had visited Stan a month before, and the two had talked excitedly, warmly, for over three hours about the one art in which they had no peer—the structuring and execution of gags.

Stan is buried in the Court of Liberty in the new Hollywood Hills Forest Lawn Cemetery. Above his grave a plaque reads

Stan Laurel

A Master of Comedy
his genius in the art of
humor brought gladness
to the world he loved.

It was composed by a director of the cemetery staff.

It is, of course, a perfectly appropriate epitaph. But as I stood there the last time I visited him, it seemed to me that somewhere, probably among my notes of our many conversations, there was something rather more fitting.

When I returned East, I sifted through myriad note-takings and the two hundred and fifty letters we had exchanged, looking for what I remembered vaguely as the few words suitable as perfect epitaph. After much travail, I found the words, oddly enough, in the oldest notes I had—the ones taken during our first meeting in 1953.

He had been describing the life of an English music hall performer in the first decade of the century. Performers of that time usually gave themselves or their act a provocative or vividly comic labeling—something on the order of "Bertie Bash—Just a Spot of Bother," or some such. In 1906, Stan had done this for his own act, a boy comedian, age sixteen; and for me these words, his self-description, will always remain his uniquely appropriate epitaph.

The first billing of his professional life was, like himself, simple, to the point, and without guile. It bespeaks him utterly:

STAN JEFFERSON:

HE OF THE FUNNY WAYS.

Appendix A
Leo McCarey

Leo McCarey's extant comments on Laurel and Hardy can now be found in three places: my interview; a *Cahiers du Cinéma* interview (No. 163, February 1965) by Serge Davey and Jean-Louis Noames; and two interviews given to Peter Bogdanovich in an Oral History (November 25, 1968–May 6, 1969) commissioned by the American Film Institute.

In the *Cahiers du Cinéma* interview, McCarey was either severely misquoted or showed a faltering memory. He is quoted as saying: "I made at least a hundred Laurel and Hardy films." Hardly. The total Laurel and Hardy product, 1926–51, was 105 films, and McCarey left Laurel and Hardy early in their career. The files of Hal Roach Studios show McCarey as either supervisor or writer for thirty-one Laurel and Hardy films.

McCarey is also quoted in *Cahiers du Cinéma* as saying he gave Babe Hardy his nickname. No. A Florida barber did that in 1914.

McCarey is also quoted: "[Stan] said that he was twice as good and twice as important [as Hardy], that he wrote the film and participated in its creation, while Hardy was really incapable of creating anything at all—it was astonishing that he could even find his way to the studio."

I flatly refuse to believe so nice a man as Leo McCarey would purposely misstate. Stan told me the reason he got double Hardy's salary was because quantitatively he did twice Hardy's work, not because he was "twice as good." Confirmation of this comes in the Peter Bogdanovich interview. Therein Stan is quoted as saying to McCarey that he did twice as much work as Hardy and wanted twice as much money.

And as to Stan's statement that Hardy was a virtual ignoramus—I strongly beg leave to doubt either that Stan said it or that Leo McCarey said he said it.

Appendix B
Filmography

This filmography has been compiled from a number of sources, including Stan Laurel's own scrapbooks and film listings (supplied by Tony and Lois Laurel Hawes and John McCabe), and the subsequent research of Richard W. Bann and R. E. Braff.

Films are listed in order of release.

THE SOLO FILMS

1917
Nuts in May (2 reels, Nestor)

1918
Hickory Hiram (1 reel, Nestor-Universal)
Phoney Photos (2 reels, LKO)
Who's Zoo? (2 reels, LKO)
No Place Like Jail (1 reel, Rolin-Pathé)
Huns and Hyphens (2 reels, Vitagraph)
Just Rambling Along (1 reel, Rolin-Pathé)
Bears and Bad Men (2 reels, Vitagraph)
Frauds and Frenzies (2 reels, Vitagraph)
It's Great to be Crazy (1 reel, Nestor-Universal)

1919
Do You Love Your Wife? (1 reel, Rolin-Pathé)
Hustling for Health (1 reel, Rolin-Pathé)
Hoot Mon! (1 reel, Rolin-Pathé)

1921
The Rent Collector (2 reels, Vitagraph)

1922
The Egg (2 reels, Amalgamated-Metro)
The Weak-End Party (2 reels, Amalgamated-Metro)

[An advertisement in the May 20, 1922 issue of Motion Picture News indicated that three Amalgamated-Metro Laurel two-reelers, *The Carpenter*, *The Booklegger* and *The Gardener* were "now ready," while *The Miner*, *Make it Snappy* and *Mixed Nuts* were "in preparation." While the latter — or a Laurel comedy by the same title — was released circa 1924, research has not revealed if the other five films were completed and released, nor whether titles were changed prior to release.]

The Lucky Dog (2 reels, Sun-Lite-Reelcraft), w/ Oliver Hardy

[The film was produced circa 1918-1919; extant prints appear to have been made in 1922.]

Mud and Sand (3 reels, Quality-Metro)

The Pest (2 reels, Quality-Metro)

1923

When Knights Were Cold (2 reels, Quality-Metro)
The Handy Man (2 reels, Quality-Metro)
The Noon Whistle (1 reel, Roach-Pathé)
White Wings (1 reel, Roach-Pathé)
Under Two Jags (1 reel, Roach-Pathé)
Pick and Shovel (1 reel, Roach-Pathé)
Collars and Cuffs (1 reel, Roach-Pathé)
Kill or Cure (1 reel, Roach-Pathé)
Gas and Air (1 reel, Roach-Pathé)
Oranges and Lemons (1 reel, Roach-Pathé)
Short Orders (1 reel, Roach-Pathé)
A Man About Town (1 reel, Roach-Pathé)
Roughest Africa (1 reel, Roach-Pathé)
Frozen Hearts (1 reel, Roach-Pathé)
The Whole Truth (1 reel, Roach-Pathé)
Save the Ship (1 reel, Roach-Pathé)
The Soilers (1 reel, Roach-Pathé)
Scorching Sands (1 reel, Roach-Pathé)
Mother's Joy (1 reel, Roach-Pathé)

1924

Smithy (1 reel, Roach-Pathé)
Postage Due (1 reel, Roach-Pathé)
Zeb vs. Paprika (1 reel, Roach-Pathé)
Brothers Under the Chin (1 reel, Roach-Pathé)
Near Dublin (1 reel, Roach-Pathé)
Rupert of Hee Haw (1 reel, Roach-Pathé)
Wide Open Spaces (1 reel, Roach-Pathé)
Short Kilts (1 reel, Roach-Pathé)
Mixed Nuts (2 reels, a Samuel Bischoff release)

Mandarin Mix-up (2 reels, Rock-Standard Cinema-Selznick)
Detained (2 reels, Rock-Standard Cinema-Selznick)
Monsieur Don't Care (2 reels, Rock-Standard Cinema-Selznick)
West of Hot Dog (2 reels, Rock-Standard Cinema-Selznick)

1925
Somewhere in Wrong (2 reels, Rock-Standard Cinema-Selznick)
Twins (2 reels, Rock-Standard Cinema-Selznick)
Pie Eyed (2 reels, Rock-Standard Cinema-Selznick)
The Snow Hawk (2 reels, Rock-Standard Cinema-Selznick)
Navy Blue Days (2 reels, Rock-Standard Cinema-Selznick)
The Sleuth (2 reels, Rock-Standard Cinema-Selznick)
Yes, Yes, Nanette (1 reel, Roach-Pathé; directed only)
Dr. Pyckle and Mr. Pryde (2 reels, Rock-Standard Cinema-Selznick)
Half a Man (2 reels, Rock-Standard Cinema-Selznick)
Unfriendly Enemies (1 reel, Roach-Pathé; directed only)
Moonlight and Noses (2 reels, Roach-Pathé; directed only)
Wandering Papas (2 reels, Roach-Pathé; directed only) w/ Hardy

1926
Madame Mystery (2 reels, Roach-Pathé; directed by Richard Wallace,
assisted by Laurel)
Never Too Old (2 reels, Roach-Pathé; Wallace/Laurel, as above)
The Merry Widower (2 reels, Roach-Pathé; Wallace/Laurel, as above)
Wise Guys Prefer Brunettes (2 reels, Roach-Pathé; directed only)
Atta Boy! (6 reels, Pathé)
Get 'Em Young (2 reels, Roach-Pathé)
Raggedy Rose (2 reels, Roach-Pathé; Wallace/Laurel, as above)
On the Front Page (2 reels, Roach-Pathé)

1927
Seeing the World (2 reels, Roach-Pathé)
Eve's Love Letters (2 reels, Roach-Pathé)
Now I'll Tell One (2 reels, Roach-Pathé)

1928
Should Tall Men Marry? (2 reels, Roach-Pathé)

1938
Stan was executive producer for a series of westerns starring Fred Scott
which were produced by Jed Buell and released through Spectrum.
Although nine titles were planned, only three were produced: *Knight of
the Plains*, *The Ranger's Round-Up*, and *Songs and Bullets*.

THE LAUREL AND HARDY FILMS

1926
45 Minutes from Hollywood (2 reels, silent; Roach-Pathé)

1927
Duck Soup (2 reels, silent; Roach-Pathé)
Slipping Wives (2 reels, silent; Roach-Pathé)
Love 'Em and Weep (2 reels, silent; Roach-Pathé)
Why Girls Love Sailors (2 reels, silent; Roach-Pathé)
With Love and Hisses (2 reels, silent; Roach-Pathé)
Sugar Daddies (2 reels, silent; Roach-MGM)
Sailors, Beware! (2 reels, silent; Roach-Pathé)
The Second Hundred Years (2 reels, silent; Roach-MGM)
Call of the Cuckoos (2 reels, silent; Roach-MGM)
Hats Off (2 reels, silent; Roach-MGM)
Do Detectives Think? (2 reels, silent; Roach-Pathé)
Putting Pants on Philip (2 reels, silent; Roach-MGM)
The Battle of the Century (2 reels, silent; Roach-MGM)

1928
Leave 'Em Laughing (2 reels, silent; Roach-MGM)
Flying Elephants (2 reels, silent; Roach-Pathé)
The Finishing Touch (2 reels, silent; Roach-MGM)
From Soup to Nuts (2 reels, silent; Roach-MGM)
You're Darn Tootin' (2 reels, silent; Roach-MGM)
Their Purple Moment (2 reels, silent; Roach-MGM)
Should Married Men Go Home? (2 reels, silent; Roach-MGM)
Early To Bed (2 reels, silent; Roach-MGM)
Two Tars (2 reels, silent; Roach-MGM)
Habeas Corpus (2 reels, silent; Roach-MGM)
We Faw Down (2 reels, silent; Roach-MGM)

1929
Liberty (2 reels, silent; Roach-MGM)
Wrong Again (2 reels, silent; Roach-MGM)
That's My Wife (2 reels, silent; Roach-MGM)
Big Business (2 reels, silent; Roach-MGM)
Unaccustomed As We Are (2 reels, sound; Roach-MGM)
Double Whoopee (2 reels, silent; Roach-MGM)
Berth Marks (2 reels, sound; Roach-MGM)
Men O' War (2 reels, sound; Roach-MGM)
Perfect Day (2 reels, sound; Roach-MGM)
They Go Boom (2 reels, sound; Roach-MGM)
Bacon Grabbers (2 reels, silent; Roach-MGM)
The Hoose-gow (2 reels, sound; Roach-MGM)
The Hollywood Revue of 1929 (120 minutes, sound; MGM)
Angora Love (2 reels, last silent film; Roach-MGM)

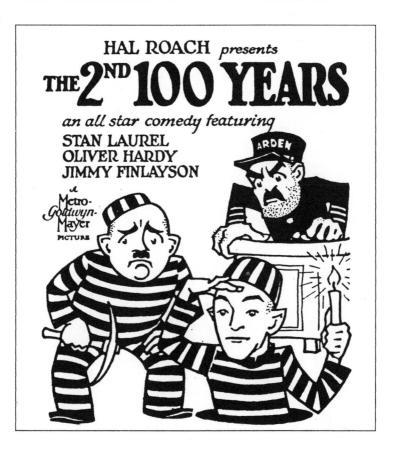

In Person

THE SCREAMS OF THE SCREEN

Stan Laurel & Oliver Hardy

FOX THE LAST WORD

WEEK STARTING FRIDAY, NOV. 22

A rare public appearance, at the new Fox Theatre in San Francisco, 1929.

1930
Night Owls (2 reels, Roach-MGM)
The Rogue Song (115 minutes, Technicolor; MGM)
Blotto (3 reels, Roach-MGM)
Brats (2 reels, Roach-MGM)
Below Zero (2 reels, Roach-MGM)
Hog Wild (2 reels, Roach-MGM)
The Laurel-Hardy Murder Case (3 reels, Roach-MGM)
Another Fine Mess (3 reels, Roach-MGM)

1931
Be Big (3 reels, Roach-MGM)
Chickens Come Home (3 reels, Roach-MGM)
The Stolen Jools (2 reels, National Variety Artists-Paramount; cameo)
Laughing Gravy (2 reels, Roach-MGM)
Our Wife (2 reels, Roach-MGM)
Pardon Us (56 minutes, Roach-MGM)
Come Clean (2 reels, Roach-MGM)
One Good Turn (2 reels, Roach-MGM)
Beau Hunks (4 reels, Roach-MGM)
On the Loose (2 reels, Roach-MGM; cameo)

1932
Helpmates (2 reels, Roach-MGM)
Any Old Port (2 reels, Roach-MGM)
The Music Box (3 reels, Roach-MGM)
The Chimp (3 reels, Roach-MGM)
County Hospital (2 reels, Roach-MGM)
Scram! (2 reels, Roach-MGM)
Pack Up Your Troubles (68 minutes, Roach-MGM)
Their First Mistake (2 reels, Roach-MGM)
Towed in a Hole (2 reels, Roach-MGM)

1933
Twice Two (2 reels, Roach-MGM)
The Devil's Brother [Fra Diavolo] (90 minutes, Roach-MGM)
Me and My Pal (2 reels, Roach-MGM)
The Midnight Patrol (2 reels, Roach-MGM)
Busy Bodies (2 reels, Roach-MGM)
Wild Poses (2 reels, Roach-MGM; cameo)
Dirty Work (2 reels, Roach-MGM)
Sons of the Desert (68 minutes, Roach-MGM)

1934
Oliver the Eighth (3 reels, Roach-MGM)
Hollywood Party (68 minutes, MGM)
Going Bye-Bye! (2 reels, Roach-MGM)
Them Thar Hills (2 reels, Roach-MGM)
Babes in Toyland (79 minutes, Roach-MGM)

The Live Ghost (2 reels, Roach-MGM)

1935
Tit for Tat (2 reels, Roach-MGM)
The Fixer Uppers (2 reels, Roach-MGM)
Thicker Than Water (2 reels, Roach-MGM)
Bonnie Scotland (80 minutes, Roach-MGM)

1936
The Bohemian Girl (70 minutes, Roach-MGM)
On the Wrong Trek (2 reels, Roach-MGM; cameo)
Our Relations (74 minutes, Roach-MGM)

1937
Way Out West (65 minutes, Roach-MGM)
Pick a Star (70 minutes, Roach-MGM)

1938
Swiss Miss (72 minutes, Roach-MGM)
Block-Heads (58 minutes, Roach-MGM)

1939
The Flying Deuces (69 minutes, Boris Morros-RKO)

1940
A Chump at Oxford (63 minutes, Roach-United Artists)
Saps at Sea (57 minutes, Roach-United Artists)

1941
Great Guns (74 minutes, 20th Century-Fox)

1942
A-Haunting We Will Go (67 minutes, 20th Century-Fox)

1943
The Tree in a Test Tube (1 reel, color; U.S. Dept. of Agriculture)
Air Raid Wardens (67 minutes, MGM)
Jitterbugs (74 minutes, 20th Century-Fox)
The Dancing Masters (63 minutes, 20th Century-Fox)

1944
The Big Noise (74 minutes, 20th Century-Fox)

1945
Nothing but Trouble (70 minutes, MGM)
The Bullfighters (69 minutes, 20th Century-Fox)

1951
Atoll K (98 minutes, Les Films Sirius; U.K. release: *Robinson Crusoeland*, 1952, Franco-London Films; U.S. release: *Utopia*, 1954, Exploitation Productions Inc. The latter two versions ran 82 minutes.)

Appendix C
"On the Spot"

This sketch, based on the Laurel and Hardy short *Night Owls*, was written for the team's 1952 tour of British music halls. It was performed under various titles, including "A Spot of Trouble," "A Spot of Bother" and "Looking for Trouble." The sketch was thought to have been lost or destroyed at the time the first edition of this book was published; it is reproduced here in its original typescript through the courtesy of Stan's daughter, Lois Laurel Hawes, and her husband Tony.

The conclusion of the sketch — which was missing at press time — is identical to *Night Owls*. The policeman who planned the phony robbery turns up on the scene just in time to get blamed for the burglary himself.

GAUMONT THEATRE - SOUTHAMPTON

Tel: 2001-2342

Manager - - H. J. EXCELL

6.15 MON. MAY 12th FOR ONE WEEK **8.30**

Matinee: SATURDAY at 2.30

HERE IN PERSON !

BERNARD DELFONT presents ————

HOLLYWOOD'S GREATEST COMEDY COUPLE

STAN   OLIVER

LAUREL AND HARDY

IN THEIR LATEST UPROARIOUS SKETCH "LOOKING FOR TROUBLE"

WITH STAR FAMILY VARIETY PROGRAMME

P.T.O.

Programme

BERNARD DELFONT

presents

STAN LAUREL and OLIVER HARDY

in

"A SPOT OF TROUBLE"

A Comedy Sketch in Two Scenes

Locale: A Small Town in the U.S.A.

Scene 1.
Waiting Room at the Railway Station

Scene 2.
The Chief of Police's Living-room

Cast:

Officer (A Small town cop with a mind smaller than the town)   LESLIE SPURLING

Chief of Police   KENNETH HENRY

Two Gentlemen En Route   **STAN LAUREL and OLIVER HARDY**

LAUREL   AND   HARDY
" ON THE SPOT. "
Comedy sketch in two scenes.
Locale: A small town in the U.S.A.

* * * * * *

ON THE SPOT
SCENE ONE

2/14/52
Page 1.

INTERIOR of Waiting Room in Railroad Station.
Cop is discovered sitting on bench, taking a nap.
Chief walks on, reading newspaper, sees Cop dozing on bench.

Chief: So -- This is where I find you - asleep on
          a public bench.

Cop: (jumps to feet saluting) Oh, hello, Chief.

Chief: This is a fine example I must say to be setting
          for our police force! Is this the way you
          perform your duty?

Cop: I was just resting my eyes.

Chief: Well, rest your eyes on this headline. Look at that!
          (holds newspaper so Cop can read it) Thirteen
          robberies in two weeks_and not one arrest. And every
          one of those robberies on your beat. The taxpayers
          of this town are plenty sore about this! They have
          already complained to the Mayor and even suggested I
          be thrown out of my job!

Cpp: But gee, Chief--

Chief: Now look, you, this is your last warning. If you
          don't snap to it, patrol your beat as you should and
          stop this wave of robbery, I'm going to throw you off
          the force! One more robbery on your beat - or even in
          this town - and you fail to catch the burglars, you're
          through -- Understand? -- You're fired!

Cop: Yes, sir.

Chief: Now get going!
          (throws paper on bench)

Both: Ad lib off.

Stan and Babe enter. Stan carries violin case containing hot
water bottle, tin cup, candle in candle-holder, binoculars, saw,
etc. Babe carries umbrella and old carpet bag. Business of
crosses and looking - sit on bench - finally see each other:
"takes".

Babe: Where have you been? I've been looking all over the
        place for you!

Stan: I was looking for you.

Babe: What for?

Stan: There was something I wanted to tell you.

Babe: What?

Stan: We missed the train.

Babe: Well, why didn't you tell me before you started to
        look for me?

Stan: Well, you always told me never to let my right hand
        know what your left foot was doing.... But maybe it's
        better we missed it anyhow.

Babe: Why?

Stan: Well, we'll be in plenty of time for the next one.

Babe: See what time's the next train.

Stan: You see what time it is.

Babe: I can't. I lost my glasses.

Stan: That's the trouble with you -- always doing something...

Stan gets binoculars out of violin case - squints through them.

Stan: I can't see through these -- something's the
        matter or something---

Babe: Here. Use one of these cleaners, then you'll be able
        to see better.

Stan: Thank you, Ollie. (wipes eyes - looks at chart on wall)
        Which way are we going -- Est or Weest?

Babe: It makes no difference. What time's the next train?

Stan: There'll be one here in ten minutes each.

Babe: Good.

Loudspeaker Voice: Oh, no there won't!
                     (Stan & Babe "take" it - voice continues)
                     Attention all passengers! Due to a storm down the
                     line a bridge has been washed out. Your train will
                     be delayed until the bridge is repaired. This will
                     take several hours. You will be notified later the
                     definite time of arrival.

Babe: Thank you.

Loudspeaker Voice: You're welcome.

Babe: Well, L guess we'll be here for the rest of the night.

Stan: Looks like we never will get home. You know -- I'm
        worried about getting on this train.

Babe: Why?

Stan: We haven't any money.

Babe: Don't, worry about that. They can't throw us off between
        stations - so we can ride to the next station free anyway.

Stan: Oh. And then they throw us off and we get on another train
        and then another one----

Babe: Exactly. And we'll be home before you can say Jack Robinson

Stan: But suppose they don't throw us off and want some money?

Babe: Tell them you'll pay them as soon as you get a job!

Stan: You think they'll wait that long?

Babe: Of course they will! These railroads are run on a very
        friendly basis.

Stan: Huh. (thoughtfully.) Say -- Who is this Jack Robinson?

Babe: Robinson Crusoe's son!

Stan: What's he got to do with it?

Babe: He hasn't got anything to do with it!

Stan: But you said he was going to get on the train and he'd get
        there before----

Babe: I didn't say he was on the train!

Leslie Spurling threatens the boys with the rockpile...or the alternative, in "On the Spot."

Cold coffee is Ollie's cup of tea — in small doses.

Stan: Well, how's he going to get there?

Babe: I don't know -- Don't ask so many questions! And stop talking

Stan: Well, if we don't talk, how are we going to pass the time
         away?

Babe: I don't know about you, but I'm going to get a little
         beauty sleep.
         (puts carpet bag on bench for pillow)

Stan: That's a good idea. I need some too.
         (Stan lays on bench - head on carpet bag Babe has fixed)

Babe: Get off of there and make your own bed!

Stan gets up - Babe lies down - Stan business with Scotch mufflers,
etc. as:

Stan: You really going to go to bed?

Babe: Yes.

Stan: Going to take your boots off?

Babe: No.

Stan: Good thing you don't wear spurs. (lights candle) -
         (by this time he has hot water bottle out - holds it up)
         How about some doffee?

Babe: No -- It's cold by now anyhow.

Stan: It shouldn't be - This is supposed to be a hot water bottle.
         (puts hot water bottle back in case, xxxxxxxxxxx takes out
         xxxxxxxxxxxxxxxx saw, business)- gets finger caught)

Babe: What's the matter now?

Stan: I can't get my finger out.

Babe: Well open the case!

         (Stan opens case, releases finger, blows out candle, puts
         it away, lies down, trying to get comfortable)

Stan: Wish they'd turn the lights off.

Babe: Why?

Stan: I can't sleep with the light on.

Babe: Put something over your eyes.

        (Stan gets newspaper from bench - places it over eyes -
        business - when all set:

Babe & Stan: "Good night" --"Good night"

Cop Enters.

Cop: Hey you! You can't sleep on there!

        (Stan and Babe get up from bench)

Babe: Pardon us, Officer.

Cop: You can't sleep in this station! What are you two doing
        here anyway?

Babe: We're waiting for a train.

Cop: Oh yeah? Well, where's your tickets?

Stan: (pointing to ticket office) In there.

Cop: You look like a couple of tramps to me!

Babe: I beg your pardon...!

Cop: Have you got any money?

Stan: We will have as soon as I get a job.

Cop: Oh, wise guy, huh! How you expect to ride on a train
        without any money?

Stan: Simple.... He says they can't throw us off between
        stations - so we can ride to the next station free - and
        then they'll throw us off -- then we can get on another
        train and they'll throw us off on our friendly basis----

Cop: Oh, just as I thought -- a couple of low down vagrants!
        Do you know what we do with tramps here?

Stan: Sure -- I saw it in a cinema.... You put them on a train
        and run them out of town. Say, Ollie, why didn't we think
        of that? It wouldn't have cost us anything.....

Cop: You're wrong! We throw them in jail for six months on the
        rock pile. (to Babe) You'll make the big rocks into little
        ones - (to Stan) And you'll make the little ones into sand!

Babe: We won't do it!

Stan: And neither will I too!

Babe: And for those insulting remarks I have a good mind to
        report you to your superior officer -- the Chief of Police
        himself!

Stan: Pérsonally...!

Cop: Say, that gives me an idea... The Chief huh?

Babe: Yes! We know our rights. We demand a hearing!

Cop: Sit down, boys -- maybe I can make a deal with you.

        (Stan whispers to Babe)

Babe: Myxxname Oh, yes. (to Cop) I'm Mr. Hardy, and this is my
        good friend Mr. Laurel.
        (business - shaking hands)

Cop: My name is Jack Robinson.

        (Bxbex& ("takes by Stan and Babe)

Stan: How's your father?

Cop: Fine, thanks. Now, how would you guys like to go free? If
        you do me a favor, I won't put you in jail. How about it?

Stan: Why sure, one good turn deserves another----

Babe: (to Stan) Just a minute. (to Cop) What's the favor?

Cop: Well, you see it's like this. (confidential) I'm in bad
        with my boss, the Chief, and I have to do something to
        square myself with him. So I want you two guys to help me
        out. All you have to do is break into the Chief's house
        tonight and pretend to rob the place. What do you think,
        chums?

Babe: (to Stan) What did he call us?

Stan: He called us chumps.

Babe: (to Cop) I resent that!

Cop: No -- no.... Not chumps - chums, pals.

Stan & Babe: Oh, that's different. -- ad lib

Cop: Now -- I'll rush in, capture you right in front of the old
        man. That will put me in his good books again and I'll be
        sitting pretty.

Babe: Yeah...But where'll we be sitting?

Stan: Oh the rock pile - with sand right up to our necks.

Cop: No, you won't! I won't even arrest you. I'll bring you both
        back here and see you safely on the train -- nice and cozy..!

Stan: Not in these trousers.

Babe: (to Cop) Are you kidding?

Cop: Certainly not. What do you say?

Babe: The deal is off.

Stan: Yes, sir, O-N-H off.

Cop: (takes out handcuffs) All right. In that case I'll lock
        you both up and it's jail for six months! Now, do you want
        the rock pile or the alternative?

Babe: Of the what?

Cop: The alternative.

Babe: Pardon me just a minute.... (to Stan) What do you think?

Stan: It depends on the difference. I might say no -- and I might
        say yes.

Cop: Good for you. (shakes Stan's hand) And you, too. (shakes
        Babe's hand) I'll show you where the place is. I'll be
        hiding right around the corner and I'll rush in and arrest
        you when I hear the signal.

Babe: What signal?

Cop: Well, when the Chief sees you, he'll more than likely take
        a shot at you and that'll be my signal.

Babe: Tell me that again.

Stan: Yes, tell us that again.

Cop: Oh, don't worry about it. When he takes a shot at you, all
        you have to do is duck. Now, pick up your junk and I'll
        wait for you outside.   (as he exits:)
        And make it snappy.

Babe: Well, here's another nice mess you got me into.

Stan: Tell him we can't do it - say we don't belong to the union.

Babe: Not a chance, if we don't go thru with it, we'll go on the
        rock pile and you'll be making enuf sand to build a new
        beach for butlin....   Come on.
            (business - letter & mail box with hand- exit BLACKOUT

Breaking into the police chief's house, in a scene borrowed from "Night Owls."

The town clock finishes striking twelve.
Scene is the Chief's living room.

SOUND: LOUD CRASH OF METAL ASH CAN.

Stan's & Babe's voices are heard o.s. - Sh-h-h each other.

Babe's Voice: Why don't you be careful? And pick up
               your big feet!   Now, look in the window
               and see if anybody is there.

Stan, carrying lighted candle, comes into view, peers thru window.

Stan: Okay, there's nobody there.

Babe: (enters scene outside window) Good. Now climb
               in the window and open the front door and let
               me in.

Babe exits towards door. Stan tries window, won't open, whistles
to Babe. Babe comes running back - "Sh-h-h!"

Stan: It's locked.

Babe: Well, do something about it!
               (starts to exit)

Stan: Say -- hand me my saw. It's in my case.

Babe hands Stan saw and exits towards door. Stan starts sawing,
making loud noise.

Babe: (enters hurriedly to Stan) Sh-h-h! You're
               making too much noise. Here - let me do it!

Babe takes saw and starts working. Stan exits towards door.
Suddenly we see the front door slowly open. Stan peeks in,
finally steps into set, closes the door quietly and locks it.
He tiptoes to the window. Babe doesn't see him as he is deeply
engrossed in his work. Stan opens catch on window and pushes
window open, which hits Babe in the face. Babe staggers out of
sight and we hear another:

SOUND: LOUD CRASH OF METAL ASH CAN

Stan looks out of window to see what has happened. Babe comes
back into sight and they "sh-h-h" each other.

Stan motions Babe to come in thru window. Babe hands him carpet
bag.

Babe: Here, take this and put everything in it.
               I'll wait for you outside.

Stan: I'm not going to rob this house alone.

Babe: Don't be selfish! Do you want us both to
               go to jail?

The Cop suddenly appears outside window, taps Babe on shoulder,
which scares Babe, and motions Babe to go on in and exits as
Babe starts to climb in.

Babe: (to Stan) Here - give me a hand.

Stan: What? - Have you changed your mind?

Babe: None of your business!

Both struggle to try and get Babe through window. Babe gets half
way thru and gets stuck.

Stan: Wait a minute -- I've got an idea.
               (he starts towards door, then returns to Babe)
               Now, don't go away.
               (starts towards door again, comes back and
                hands candle to Babe)
               Hold this.

Babe: Put it down somewhere!

Stan places candle on small table by door and then exits thru
front door, closing it after him. He then enters to window, in
back of Babe and starts trying to lift and push Babe in.

Stan: Now - Ups-a-daisy.

Babe: Don't get fancy! Just get me in here!

Babe finally gets thru window and in doing so, grabs one of the
curtains, which pulls one side of it to the floor. Stan exits
towards door. As Babe gets himself untangled from the curtain
there is a knock on the door. Babe starts to look out window for
Stan as the doorbell rings.

SOUND: DOORBELL RINGING

Babe rushes to door, opens it and in walks Stan.

Stan: Thank you, Ollie.

Babe kicks Stan in the fanny.

Stan: What's that for?

Babe: We'll discuss that later. Now put that
               curtain back up there!

Stan: (makes attempt to put curtain up)
               I can't reach it.

Babe: Stand on my back.

Babe gets down on all fours. Stan starts to climb on his back.

Babe: (gives groan) Ow-w-w! Take those big
               boots off!

Stan starts to take his boots off but notices the table standing
near the window, gets an idea. He places the table over Babe
without Babe's knowledge and climbs up on the table then looks
down at Babe.

Stan: How's that?

Babe: That's much better without your boots.

Stan starts fiddling with the curtain, trying to fix it.

Babe: Hurry up -- I can't hold you much longer.

Stan: Don't worry -- I'll have it up before
               you can say Jack Robinson.

Babe: Never mind Jack Robinson! Just hurry and
               get it up there!

Cop: (looks in window) Did you call me?

Stan: Uh - uh.

Cop exits. Stan finally gets the curtain up, gets off table,
removes it from over Babe and puts it back in place.

Stan: Okay.

Babe: (as he is getting up - Stan helping him)
               Oh..... My poor back!

Babe picks up carpet bag and motions for Stan to get silverware.
At this point the phone bell rings. (The phone is on the sideboard)

SOUND: PHONE BELL

Stan, not thingk thinking, walks over to phone and picks up receiver as Babe goes to front door and looks out.

Stan: (into phone) Hello.

Babe turns, exasperated, "shushes" him, as Stan realizes, puts
receiver back on hook. Babe hides behind window drape. Stan
goes to hide with him. Babe pushes him out.

Two minds without a single thought.

Index

Index

Index

Index

Also Available from Moonstone Press

LAUREL AND HARDY: THE MAGIC BEHIND THE MOVIES
by Randy Skretvedt • Foreword by Steve Allen
This behind-the-scenes documentary on the beloved comedy team tells how they made their classic comedies, and what happened during the making of them. Exclusive interviews and rare photographs.

"Not only the best book on Laurel and Hardy ever assembled but also one of the best books on film comedy and Hollywood..."
— *Kirkus Reviews*

SPIKE JONES AND HIS CITY SLICKERS
By Jordan R. Young • Foreword by Dr. Demento
The unauthorized biography of the legendary bandleader-comedian, who parlayed his cowbell-hiccup-and-gunshot renditions of popular songs into fame and fortune.

"A treasurable piece of nostalgia... Record collectors will appreciate the lengthy discography."   — *Booklist*

REEL CHARACTERS: GREAT MOVIE CHARACTER ACTORS
by Jordan R. Young • Foreword by Fritz Feld
Home video and cable TV have brought these unforgettable faces from Hollywood's Golden Era into millions of homes: twelve of Hollywood's best loved supporting players.

"Photographs are copiously spread throughout the text, and the filmography for each actor is very detailed, including unbilled bits..."   — *Library Journal*

LET ME ENTERTAIN YOU
by Jordan R. Young • Foreword by Leonard Maltin
Candid interviews with some of the top names in the entertainment world — discussing their careers, their successes and failures, their talents and shortcomings — are the focus of this fascinating book.

"Glimpses of performers with their guards — and egos — lowered... younger readers will learn, older ones will reminisce and enthusiasts will enjoy."   — *Publishers Weekly*

ORDERING INFORMATION ON REVERSE

Order Form

Please send the following books:

Qty		Amount
_____	*Comedy World of Stan Laurel* paperback @ $12.95	_____
_____	*Laurel and Hardy* paperback @ $14.95	_____
_____	*Laurel and Hardy* limited hardcover @ $24.95	_____
_____	*Spike Jones* paperback @ $14.95	_____
_____	*Spike Jones* limited hardcover @ $19.95	_____
_____	*Reel Characters* paperback @ $9.95	_____
_____	*Reel Characters* limited hardcover @ $19.95	_____
_____	*Let Me Entertain You* paperback @ $9.95	_____

Total for books _____

Postage: add $1.75 for first book, .50 each additional _____

California residents please add 6% tax _____

Amount enclosed (U.S. funds) _____

Ship to:

_____

_____

_____

IF THIS IS A LIBRARY BOOK, PLEASE PHOTOCOPY THIS PAGE.
ALL OUR BOOKS ARE PRINTED ON ACID-FREE PAPER.
SATISFACTION GUARANTEED OR PURCHASE PRICE REFUNDED.

MOONSTONE PRESS
P.O. Box 142 • Beverly Hills CA 90213